THE INSIDER'S GUIDE
TO BUYING A
NEW OR USED CAR

BURKE LEON &
STEPHANIE LEON

BETTERWAY BOOKS
CINCINNATI, OHIO

Acknowledgments

Thanks to Mike and Tom at Advantage Auto for helping me get into the business and for giving me insights that I wouldn't have obtained any other way. Thanks also for being our friends.

As our readers will find out, I (Burke) am the technical guru behind this book. Even though I know what to say, I needed a lot of help in writing and organizing the material in this book. Stephanie is not an auto expert, but she knows how to take my thoughts and translate them into prose. For those of you who are planning on writing a book with someone else, think well on the subject. If that person is your wife, lover, mother of your children, and also your critic, you could lose the remainder of your hair over it. Thank you, Stephanie.

Typography by Blackhawk Typesetting

The Insider's Guide to Buying a New or Used Car. Copyright © 1993 by Burke Leon and Stephanie Leon. Printed and bound in the United States of America. All rights reserved. No part of this book may be reproduced in any form or by any electronic or mechanical means including information storage and retrieval systems without permission in writing from the publisher, except by a reviewer, who may quote brief passages in a review. Published by Betterway Books, an imprint of F&W Publications, Inc., 1507 Dana Avenue, Cincinnati, Ohio 45207. 1-800-289-0963. First edition.

---

97 96 95 94   5 4 3 2

Library of Congress Cataloging-in-Publication Data

Leon, Burke.
   The insider's guide to buying a new or used car : hundreds of tips in easy to use checklist format from a veteran insider / Burke Leon and Stephanie Leon.
      p. cm.
   Includes index.
   ISBN 1-55870-284-9 : $9.95
   1. Automobiles — Purchasing. 2. Consumer education.   I. Leon, Stephanie . II. Title.
   TL162.L46 1993
   629.222'0297—dc20   92-38567
                                                           CIP

To my twenty-two year old son, Andrew, who taught me everything he knows about the auto business.

To my nineteen year old son, Stephen, who gave up his summer and fall in 1993 to help start B.L. Auto Enterprises in Ontario. Thanks kiddo, we couldn't have done it without you.

CONTENTS

Introduction: How This Book was Born

The single question I'm asked most often is, "How did a nice, honest, professional like you get into a grubby business like this?" While I do have a lifelong interest in games and human psychology and have developed an interest in being savvy and coming out a winner in negotiated settlements, I did not spend my life preparing to be an auto dealer, an auto salesman, or a consumer auto expert.

I went through high school in a small town in upstate New York taking a college entrance program. I breezed through college with a B.S. in chemistry, an M.S. in inorganic chemistry, and eventually a Ph.D. in physical chemistry. My Ph.D. thesis was entitled, "Magnetic Coupling and Phase Boundaries for some C15 and C22 'Pseudo Binary' Alloys Containing Lanthanides."

When I was in school, I took one of the most difficult curricula around; calculus, physics, chemistry, etc. — no basket weaving for me. Yet every time I needed something non-academic, I had to put out at least 150% effort while some of these slippery-slidy guys effortlessly got the most sought-after prizes — and the best-looking women until I met my present wife and co-author Stephanie. Somehow, things came more easily to them. They could talk their ways into things I had to work hard for and *still* couldn't get. Even more important, they could talk their way out of things with equal ease. If one of them asked me for favors, I would almost always oblige. About the only things at which I could beat them (other than intellectual pursuits) were games for money such as poker and bridge, where I *really* knew the rules.

It was later in life when I realized that, highly trained in our specialties as we intellectuals might be, we are *grossly untrained* in handling people and in negotiating situations — and these situations have enormous monetary paybacks. Not only aren't we trained to negotiate, we are trained *not* to negotiate. There will be more on this later.

One of the advantages of being a reasonably well-paid scientific professional during the heyday of science was that I didn't have to worry about monetary paybacks. I could ignore how lower-level technicians were making hundreds or thousands of dollars on the side by buying, fixing up, and selling cars in their spare time. I was a scientist, not a technician, a big social and economic difference. I could just go out, pay sticker price (get taken), and it didn't hurt my pocketbook too badly.

My interest in how to negotiate for cars got a start when the company I worked for in New York went under. I hung around Huntington Station, Long Island for a couple of months before I realized that the job market wasn't going to recover anytime in the foreseeable future. So I called on some old friends and landed in Orange County, California in their economic boom times. Before I left for Orange County (right next to L.A.), I knew I was going to have to buy a new car. Frankly I was still nursing bad vibes from my last buy(s). Now, however, for the first time, money *was* a problem. I had to do better at car buying this time.

I decided that never again would I be out of control in a car-buying situation — never ever-ever-ever. So I went to my local bookstore, checked out every book ever written on how to buy a car, and engineer-like, sat down and read them all from cover to cover — taking notes. At the end of the reading sessions, I said, "So *that's* how they do it!" and "So, *that's* what I did wrong!" and "Boy, was I dumb!" After that reading, I realized that those people (new car dealers) could never do it to me again. I knew then that I would get my revenge when I bought my next car. And I did. I "killed" them on my next new car buy and here's how I did it.

MY FIRST REVENGE

Picture the scene: I went to California first and was waiting for my wife to sell our home in New York. My company car allowance was about to run out, and now was the time to get a new car. I had to act quickly. At first, I didn't know what I wanted, but I finally narrowed it down to two: a Ford Taurus and a Dodge Lancer. I liked the Taurus; my wife liked the Lancer. Guess who won.

The conversation at the dealership went something like this:
SALESPERSON: Why don't you just buy the Lancer?
ME: I don't know if my wife would like it, she hasn't seen it.
SALESPERSON insinuates, "Be a man. Make up your mind and just do it."
ME: I really want some input from my wife.
SALESPERSON: So why don't you call her and get her input?

So I did. I made a 20-minute long-distance call from Orange County, California to Huntington Station, New York for my wife's input—on the dealership's bill. Eventually I bought the Lancer and we loved it.

The buy took place on the last day of the month, a Sunday, after a rainy holiday weekend and started in a near empty showroom at 9:00 P.M. — one hour before closing.

The buy ended at 1:00 A.M. with no one shaking hands with me or telling me what a good deal I got. Sixty seconds after I drove out of the dealership with my new car, the place was deserted. They were tired and couldn't wait to get away.

During the course of the negotiation, the salesperson switched from price, to payments, to leasing, to value, to don't-we-have-to-make-a-profit? I brought along an extra party, someone from work, whose only job was to get in the way — and he did. The dealership sales staff (at the end, there were four people trying to wrap it up) still couldn't figure out what he was doing there or how to handle me. My repetition of, "I really want to buy a car tonight," and "Why won't you let me buy a car tonight?" kept them interested when it looked as if we would deadlock.

I started off negotiating for a bare-bones Dodge Lancer and eventually settled for what I really wanted, a year-old, brand new, fully loaded Lancer ES with only twenty-five original miles and a very, very small dent in the fender. The price also dropped from an asked $15,200 to $9,995 with a special low-interest package. Ten days later, they tried to get a higher interest rate by saying the bank wouldn't approve me. I told them to take back the car and amazingly, the bank approved me.

It wasn't easy to negotiate the first time, but I did it — and did it well. I did it so well that when others in my company heard about it, they asked me to negotiate for a new car for them. Now this is a part of my business.

I "did cars" for other people, and each time I got better at it. I also found that it was not enough just to tell people how to buy a car. Soon I was organizing my thoughts; writing things down. Someone suggested that I give a course. As of this writing, I have given over ninety courses on "How to Buy a Car" and "How to Negotiate" at five different colleges. I have also appeared as a guest expert on television.

It was after the television appearance that I started thinking about what all experts envision — "THE BOOK." A good book would help others organize their car-buying experience by supplying all the relevant information. The book would include lists that are crucial for a good buy and would be organized to be useful at each stage of the car buying process. It would need to be easy for the reader to access the information. This book is meant to be organized for your convenience. I hope you find it easy to use, especially under the pressure of an actual auto buy. It is intended to make that job easier.

It is everybody's dream to drive into a dealership in their old car, toss the keys to a salesperson, point to a fully-loaded dream car, pay the asking price with a roll of hundreds, and drive out fifteen minutes later with all the paperwork done. Well, that happens only in your dreams; it is never so simple.

AUTO BOOKS

There are a lot of good books on the market telling you about how to buy a car. *Cheap Wheels* by Sachs and Bennett is almost 300 pages long and contains lots of information on how to evaluate used cars, but doesn't tell the reader how to negotiate for a car. If you already know how to buy a car, the book provides very helpful information on mechanical evaluation and warnings about potential scams.

The Car Buyer's Art by Darrell Parrish has close to 150 pages and tells the new car buyer what to do and how to do it. The book provides interesting and entertaining stories, but the information is not presented in a way that is immediately usable.

There are a lot of other good books on the market which I am sure some of you will read and enjoy. But *reading* about car buying is one thing; understanding it is another, being successful at it is still another, and doing a great job of buying a car is an art form.

The basic problem with buying a car well is that most Americans simply are not trained to do it. Most of us grow up with only one negotiating style: "take it or leave it." Hard, rude, brutal, face-to-face negotiation is foreign and frightening to us. The ideal way to learn to negotiate for a car would be at the side of an expert car buyer who would lead you through the transaction, protect you from the big bad car salesperson, and, like a good coach, tell you what you did wrong and critique you later. This almost never happens. You mostly bleed and learn nothing. You most certainly leave feeling demoralized and battered.

No matter how diligently you read the books on "How to Buy a Car," it is not enough. Theoretical knowledge alone won't do it. You need other kinds of help to hold your own with a car dealer on his own turf. Having some buying experience and a strong personality is, of course, helpful. If you have neither and you can't get someone who is competent to go with you to help with the negotiations, the next best thing is to have detailed checklists of what to do and how to do it at each stage of the buying process and to live and die by this well-thought-out plan. I have yet to see this in other books on this subject. They simply do not provide this vital information in a form that is easily extractable. This book is designed to provide user-friendly guides and lists to ensure that you get the car you want at the best possible price.

People who do things well in any field usually have either a mental or a written plan that they follow. When you go grocery shopping, you take a shopping list. When you close a business deal, you have a checklist of items that must be settled before you sign. When you buy a car you also need an expert's list of items to discuss and to act upon. Other car-buying books give you items to consider; none of them give you usable lists to follow and act upon.

The lists in this book are designed to work. They are specific enough to be practical and useful, and general enough to apply to all car buyers. Obviously, they may not cover every situation for every person, but they will assist a well-informed, well-prepared consumer. I encourage you to add special or personalized items that will help you.

This book is organized to help you. It sets the stage for your purchase by answering the questions most people ask. It then helps you assess your automotive needs and decide what you can afford with lists that help you focus your priorities. It provides detailed lists to help you complete important homework assignments like finding and comparing research evaluating your car choice and filling out rating sheets, locating financing, and pricing the worth of your trade-in. After doing your homework, you will be shown the four parts of any automobile transaction and the exact order in which to execute them.

The book will then discuss various aspects of buying a new car and provide organizational information and checklists to make sure you stay on track. All of the information presented is direct and practical.

There are chapters discussing topics from creating the right buying attitude, to financing, to getting the best price for your trade-in. You will also be told what advantages the dealerships have and what strengths you possess as a buyer. This will enable you to maximize your strong points and negate theirs. You will then be introduced to the techniques of the sales professionals and learn how to counter them. This information is critical if you are to maintain the best possible negotiating position.

In my work, I eventually looked beyond new cars and found a whole new world in the buying of used cars. I share this with you in Section II. It should become apparent to you after reading these chapters that late model used cars bought at dealers only auctions are the best of all possible deals, bar none.

The last few chapters deal with how to sell a car yourself, the right questions to ask when buying a car from a private party, and screening calls from potential buyers over the telephone. This is hard core practical information that nobody else shows you.

Dig into the book, personalize the lists, and bring home a great car deal. If you do a magnificent job, or have questions or suggestions for personalizing the lists or improving the book, please feel free to call or write me at the address and phone number below.

By the time you read this, I will have completed audio tapes on "How to Buy a Car." If you want information or if you want to order these tapes, write to me. I am a great lecturer, funny, fast paced and very informative — these will be excellent tapes. I am available to answer questions about the automobile market in general or to give specific advice on automobiles and price quotations. In addition, I am available to lecture on subjects related to automobiles and negotiation.

If you have any special topics that you feel need addressing in this book, please call or write and let me know what you think is important, timely, pertinent or of interest. I will try to insert your information — if you want — with a "thank you," in the next edition of this book.

B.L. Auto Enterprises
750 W. Holt Blvd.
Ontario, CA 91762
(714)996-2075

Section I:
How to Buy a New Car

Setting the Stage for the Car-Buying Process

People often feel so overwhelmed by the complexity of the car-buying process that they just follow the direction of the salesperson in order to avoid confusion. The following list of questions and answers should give you enough information to allow you to feel more confident. These are the questions people considering buying a car ask me most frequently, followed by my response.

Why is buying a car so complex?

The system is specifically designed to make it difficult, confusing, painful, and protracted — for you — and profitable for the car company. The car-buying system is set up to extract the maximum money from you by confusing you, tempting you, and finally, wearing you out.

It is true that there are a lot of items that must be decided upon, but making these decisions easy for you is not as high on the dealer's list of priorities as maximizing his profits at each step of the transaction. Unlike buying most retail items where there is a marked price to which only tax can be added, there are lots of ways in which the salesperson and dealership can add to their profits at the moment of the sale.

Why does buying a car take so long?

There are several reasons:

♦ Many people don't really know their own minds. They don't know if they really want or can afford a new car; thus, it becomes relatively easy to confuse and manipulate them.

♦ Almost no one has any idea what his trade-in is worth, and most buyers are depending on that money to use as the down payment on their new car.

♦ Most people have not decided which car, model, or accessories they want. Evaluating the various options takes time.

♦ Both salesperson and customer are determined to take whatever time and trouble are necessary to get the best deal. Usually the salesperson can wait the customer out.

♦ Getting financing is not always easy, even with good credit. Calculating the amount of down payments, cash back, etc., takes time even under the best of circumstances.

♦ Doing all the paperwork and explaining all the legalities is time consuming.

Not only does the average person have to go through all of the above, he has to do them so well that he gets everything he wants and needs with a minimum of grief. Here is where good negotiating skills come in.

Why do most of us have so much trouble negotiating for a car?

Americans are not trained in how to negotiate. In most cases they find negotiating distasteful. In the good old United States, down and dirty negotiating, head-to-head bickering, and fighting over money seem to have a connotation of being lower class, or at the very least petty. Unlike people from other countries, Americans just have not learned how to negotiate well and with class since they usually don't do any negotiating at all. On everyday items — groceries, mortgage, light bills, and library fines — the "take it or leave it" rule is never questioned. We rarely negotiate for anything.

There are only two exceptions; it is deemed okay to bicker for houses and cars. While both of these are really big ticket items that will force you to pay for any costly mistakes for years, there are some major differences in the way they are handled. On the whole, you are much better protected and represented when buying a house than you are when buying a car.

When you are buying a house, you don't have to present the bid face to face; you do so through a third party, the Realtor. He carries your bid to the seller, then carries the seller's response back to you, and then back and forth as necessary. When the time comes to sign, your lawyer is there to represent your interests. On the whole, it is a very impersonal process designed to keep the buyers and sellers apart — so they don't ruin the deal the professionals have set up (and depend upon for their livelihood).

Car negotiation doesn't work that way. You, an amateur, go head-to-head in a small room with a practiced professional who is pressuring you to buy a car — *today*. There is no one there to make sure that you are not being taken advantage of. In fact, there are many people there who will tell you what a good deal you are getting, although just the opposite is true. Is it any wonder that so many people find negotiating for a car so distasteful that they usually end up paying more than they can afford just to end the transaction?

What is a fair amount of money to allow a dealership to make on an auto sale?

I thought you would never ask. The best way to ask that question is not how *much* profit, but how *little* profit should I allow them to make. Why be concerned with their profits and not your own when dealerships only concern themselves with maximizing their profits? After you have read this book, you will be able to calculate things like dealer's cost in order to make your best offer on a car. The only question you should be asking is, "How little can I give to a dealership to get the car I want?"

In hard times, dealers can be beaten down in price quite easily. But car sales, like most economic transactions, follow the laws of supply and demand. In times when cars are "scarce," dealers are much tougher to deal with. "Rare" cars and special edition cars also will go for a premium price. Consider the Mazda Miata. When it was first introduced, it was going for as much as $4000 over list. A year later, when Mazda was in full production, the price was discounted from the MSRP (Manufacturers Suggested Retail Price), or list price.

Here is a good rule of thumb: the more expensive the car, the more profit is built in. Hence there is more latitude for obtaining a hefty discount on a luxury car. The following is a rough but realistic guide to go by when trying to limit dealership profit.

CAR PRICE	PROFIT TO ALLOW THE DEALER
LESS THAN $10,000	$200-$300
$10,000-$14,000	$300-$500
$14,000-$19,000	$400-$600
$19,000-$23,000	$600-$700

Why are high pressure sales tactics the rule?

The salesperson is working on commission. He gets a percentage of the dealer's profits. The higher price you pay, the more expensive car you buy, the more options he sells; the more money he makes. In addition, he has weekly sales quotas to meet. His job is at stake. The finance and insurance (F & I) person also gets paid as a percentage of the amount of money he makes on the "back end" or financing part of the transaction. That's why it is not surprising that he tries very hard to sell you upgrade stereo systems, long-term warranties, or anti-theft packages. Other people get paid similarly for their part in the transaction.

In addition, the salesperson knows that if the sale isn't closed today, he probably won't get another chance. You won't be back tomorrow, no matter how sincerely you try to convince him that you need more time to think it over. Statistically, only 3% to 6% of auto customers ever come back to the same salesperson and he knows it. This increases the pressure on him tremendously.

What do you recommend buying? A new or used car?

There are advantages to both. But there are some great bargains to be had in used cars as compared to new cars. The ideal kind of used car to buy is one with only a few thousand miles on it (1+ years old with about 12,000 to 18,000 miles). In this case you would have a nearly new car at a much lower price because new cars can drop 40% in value during their first year of operation.

This great loss of value immediately after purchase is reason to strongly consider buying a low mileage used car as the best of all possible deals. Even preferable to that is buying a low mileage used car at a dealers only auction. Auction buying of a nearly new used car is the best of all possible worlds. (There is more on this in the second section of the book.)

When should I consider buying a new car?

Usually this comes up when your old car is worth very little and is in need of costly repairs. From my personal experience, cars of the '70s and early '80s were essentially ready to be traded in after about three years and 50,000 miles. The newer cars are good for a longer period of time, and with the long-term warranties on power trains and engines, they will serve you well much longer — so long that you may well get bored with your car before it gets terminally ill. Most people now get a new vehicle when they are bored with their old one or when it no longer serves its original purpose.

Are there advantages to leasing?

Even statisticians can't make up their minds whether leasing is a better deal than installment buying. But they all agree that *leasing is a great marketing tool*. In general, leasing is better if you don't have enough money for a large down payment and you want smaller monthly payments. For this reason, it is an easier sale. Sales staff can stress the lower monthly payments, and of course forget to tell you that it is possible for you to negotiate for all sorts of things — exactly as you would when buying the same car. Typically, both the payments and the down payment are lower in a lease. Because of this, the salesperson experiences less sales resistance, *even though the customer is getting a worse deal*. The bottom line is that car dealers find it easier to make larger profits on leasing. Manufacturers support leasing because most leases run for three years as compared to an average of five years for an installment buy. This means that car shoppers will be looking for new cars two years earlier if they lease. This two-year difference in turnaround means that Detroit makes more sales.

There is one additional item that you consider if you lease; most problems occur at the end of the lease, while on a cash or installment buy the problems occur at the beginning. With a lease, you have to pay for extra mileage, damage to the car, cracked glass, ripped seats, and a variety of end-of-the-lease fees *when the car is turned in*. In a buy, all the extra costs are put on the front end of the buy so you know the damages immediately rather than being surprised at the end.

Many people choose leasing because they think it is easier than buying. If you are returning a lease and leaving with a new lease, there is no hassle over trade-in price, typically the worst part of a car buy. There is also no ownership in leasing so there are fewer worries about the car being a lemon or not running well over the long term. You don't have to think (worry) about selling your car, because you never own it.

Leasing has so many good points in terms of convenience and simplicity that people are willing to pay way too much more for a leased car. Why? Because the costs aren't apparent until the end, there is no trade-in hassle, and both the monthly and down payments are smaller. I believe the average person ultimately pays less to buy but may have more complications at the front end of the buy than they have at the front end of leasing.

Which are better, American or foreign cars?

No one should buy American just to support Detroit. Those people won't buy American just to support you. GM, Ford, and Chrysler got into trouble because they made bad decisions, let quality slip, thought the American consumer would never buy a foreign car, and didn't recognize the formidable competition that was rising in Europe and especially in Japan.

For the past fifteen years, Japanese cars have put together a great combination of quality and price. Ten to fifteen years ago there was a huge quality gap between foreign built and American built cars. But today, *Consumer Reports* indicates that the quality gap is very small. Don't discount American cars out of hand just because they had quality problems in 1981. Quality today is not enough of an issue to mandate a "buy foreign" attitude.

The overall consideration should be, "How can I get the most for my buck?" Since American cars are selling at discounts and Japanese cars are selling at a premium, the best deal is to get a suitable car at a great price. This is possible now because American dealers are more willing to deal. Today, due to their increased popularity and reputation, it is difficult to negotiate for Japanese cars. The rising value of the Japanese yen in the fall of 1993 will make American cars much more price attractive than Japanese cars. American cars will be excellent bargains since the prices will be lower and the quality will be comparable to the Japanese.

This illustrates what a decade or so of lean financial profits can do to Detroit's disposition. Buy American if it suits you, if the quality is good, and especially if the price is right. If you feel the quality or the design or the sales and service are still inadequate, give them another decade of "lean cuisine" to get their act together.

Do sales staff have the ability to make a sale without the approval of their managers?

Not generally, and for a good reason. Sales staff come and go and often are not highly regarded by their bosses. The real power in the dealership is the closer or sales manager. He or she has the ability to say yes or no to a deal. If you want to really see this, ask the salesperson in your next car deal, "Do you have the authority to make a deal without consulting your boss?" He may say yes, but most likely he won't answer the question. Press him for an answer and you will find that at best he can only sell you a car for sticker price. He is just there to wear you down until a real salesperson, "the closer," can finish the sale.

Is it possible for the average person to read a book, become an instant expert, and buy a car like a pro?

Probably not, but you can come close by following an expertly derived plan or system using checklists. This system must be executed by a knowledgeable consumer. You can become a knowledgeable consumer only by doing your homework.

Homework is the subject of the next chapter — what homework to do, different types of assignments, and lists to help you do them.

2

Doing Your Homework

Let me set the stage for the kind of homework I expect you to do. I say this at all the classes I teach on the subject of "How to Buy a Car." There is perhaps $2000 in "profits" that either can be saved by you or can be given to the dealership. The lion's share of this will go to the dealership if you *don't* do your homework. The lion's share will be saved by you if you do the homework and follow the directions in this book. Doing a buy right will require about twenty hours of very pleasurable work. This means that you will make about $2000 in about twenty hours of work, or about $100 per hour. This is, of course, after taxes, so to generate this kind of money conventionally, you must make about $150 per hour before taxes. If you were going to pay someone this kind of money to buy a car for you, you would expect a hard-working, dedicated person who did her homework and did the buying well. This is exactly what I expect from you and what you should expect from yourself.

There are two general categories that must be considered: "HOME-WORK" items and items listed as "AT THE DEALERSHIP." The HOME-WORK items can be done in advance and in any order, but the items under "AT THE DEALERSHIP" *must* be done in the order given or you will lose control of the buy. Any time you lose control of the buy, you will lose money. That should be incentive for doing your homework and following the prescribed order once you are at the dealership.

HOMEWORK

These can be done in any order, but must be done *before* your trip to the dealership to look at cars.

Read About the Cars You Are Considering

Ready, set, go. Start with *Consumer Reports* for information about costs and reliability. Next try *Road and Track* or *Car and Driver* to see how the experts like the vehicle and what specific options and equipment they recommend. Look at other magazines and publications and go on from there. Start now.

SUGGESTED INFORMATION SOURCES

♦ Edmund's Publications Corp.
515 Hempstead Turnpike
Hempstead, New York 11552
(516)292-0044

Edmund's publishes a variety of useful guides. These guides cover new car prices for most classes of cars and trucks, including: domestic cars and trucks, foreign cars and trucks, and some used car prices. These guides cost around $5.00 each and are updated once or twice yearly. Edmund's is a great source of information. You might find it useful to buy the guide that deals specifically with the type of car you need.

♦ *NADA (National Automobile Dealers Association) Official Used Car Guide*, commonly called the "Blue Book." This great source of used car price evaluations has page upon page of price information about all sorts of used cars. It makes no recommendations, just acts as a reflection of the current market value. The purpose of the Blue Book is to report current market prices for automobiles, not to set them.

When dealers talk among themselves, they refer to the Blue Book very often. Rather than saying, "I will buy that car for $5300," a dealer might say, "I will buy that car for $800 under Book."

Do not take the Blue Book prices as gospel. Many factors, including condition, color, and local availability can seriously affect the price.

♦ *Consumer Reports*, especially the annual automobile issue that comes out each April. I look to *Consumer Reports* for very good information about reliability and repair records. They also have a whole raft of books on various aspects of car buying.

♦ Auction reports for dealers only auctions. These reports are sent only to authorized dealers, so while you cannot get them directly, you might be able to work with a dealer who has them. These reports report the sales prices at the dealers only auction. They let me know very vividly what cars sell for at these auctions. These types of reports are what the Blue Book is in part based upon.

Some good books that I have read on the subject of car buying include:

♦ *The Car Buyer's Art* by Darrell Parrish (Book Express, 1985).

♦ *Cheap Wheels* by Leslie R. Sachs and James S. Bennett (Simon & Schuster, 1989).

- *How to Buy a Car* by James R. Ross (St. Martin's Press, 1988).
- *How to Buy a New Car* by Thomas E. Bonsall (Bookman Publishing, 1989).
- *How to Save Big Money When You Lease a Car* by Michael Flinn (Putnam Publishing, 1989).

Choose Which Car and Options to Buy

This part of your homework includes pricing options like stereos and anti-theft systems at outside sources. Use the checklists at the end of this chapter to help you think your way through all the available choices. Determine what your needs are versus what your wants are. Prioritize, then get a rough idea of what you can afford and figure out what your payments will be.

Get Your Financing in Order

Chapters 15 and 16 of this book will be useful in helping you sort through the financing maze. Go to a bank, credit union, and/or your favorite relative and get your financing in shape *before* you go into the dealership. Make sure you are approved for enough money at a good interest rate and make sure that it will be available when you want it. It is a horror to lose a car or to pay top financing interest rates because your loan falls through or because you haven't financed enough to cover the car you really want. It is also a horror if your loan falls through because you buy a car through an auction and *then* discover that your lending institution doesn't loan on auction purchases. Get all the details of your loan or financing straightened out and completely in order *before* the buy.

Price Your Trade-In

Chapter 4 provides you with help in evaluating your vehicle. Chapters 9, 22, and 23 will give you valuable information on what you can get for it in a dealership or by selling it yourself through advertisements. Don't dismiss selling a car yourself without thinking the process through via this book. It may not "be for you" to sell it yourself, but then again it might make you some serious extra money.

Pick the Dealership

I first consider only those dealerships that are close and therefore convenient. It is important that they be large enough to offer discounts more easily. In addition, I check for reputation, longevity, and consider the success of the dealership in fulfilling repair warranties.

Pick the Time and a Buying Companion

As you will see in Chapter 5 and elsewhere, your advantages as a buyer are strongly influenced by picking the best time (end of the month, rainy weekend, late in the day, shortly before closing) and having the right people with you. Don't go when it is convenient for the dealership. Go when it makes sense for you to get a great deal.

Practice

If the opportunity presents itself, go with a friend to his car buy and practice. Help him with his buy and use the experience gained for your benefit. Practice makes perfect: if you make mistakes, make them before your purchase.

AT THE DEALERSHIP

Remember, these items must be executed *in the order listed* for you to maintain control of the sales situation. These things are done at the dealership with the sales staff *after* all of the homework items have been completed. Each of these steps is discussed in detail in later chapters.

♦ Meet the salesperson and take a test drive.
♦ Get a fixed firm price for your trade-in.
♦ Set a fixed firm price for the new car and options.
♦ Settle all the financing issues, including payments, leasing, extended warranties, etc.

CHECKLISTS

What Kind of Car Do You Want and Need?

Deciding what kind of car you need and want means searching your soul and your wallet and examining your dreams, reasons, and motivations. It is also the most important thing to do before you step into a dealership. The purpose of this section is to help you focus on what you really want or need in a vehicle.

Winging it may be fun, but it is seldom profitable. One of the problems with going to a dealership unprepared is that if you really aren't settled on what type of car you want, the salesperson will certainly help you make up your mind. That usually means switching you to the particular car that is the most profitable for him to sell. If his dealership is offering incentives to sales staff for selling luxury cars, you will be pressed to buy one of them. You may go out to buy a station wagon and come back with a sports car. The best way to avoid this kind of pressure is to make up your mind logically and carefully in your own home. Filling out this form will help you.

This Car Will Be Used For:

_____ driving to work
_____ hauling cargo
_____ hauling kids and groceries
_____ impressing the neighbors
_____ improving better social life (sports car)
_____ long distance commuting
_____ sales calls
_____ other _____
_____ other _____
_____ other _____

I Need a Car with the Following Characteristics:

_____ lots of economy
_____ lots of luxury
_____ lots of power
_____ lots of room
_____ holds ___ people easily
_____ 2, 4, 5 doors
_____ other_____
_____ other_____
_____ other_____
_____ other_____

	WANT	NEED	COMMENTS (PRO/CON)
1. luxury car			
2. minivan			
3. recreation vehicle			
4. sedan 4-door			
5. sedan 2-door			
6. sports car			
7. station wagon			
8. truck			
9. other			

CONCLUSIONS ABOUT WHAT KIND OF CAR I NEED:

_____

_____

_____

Here is a sample of the completed checklist:

		WANT	NEED	COMMENTS (PRO/CON)
1.	luxury car	yes	no	too expensive
2.	minivan	no	no	useful, but…
3.	recreation vehicle	yes	no	too expensive
4.	sedan 4-door	yes	yes	boring, but I need a four-door family car
5.	sedan 2-door	no	no	need 2nd set of doors
6.	sports car	desperately	none	can't afford
7.	station wagon	no	no	not useful to me
8.	truck	yes	no	fun, but…
9.	other			

CONCLUSIONS ABOUT WHAT KIND OF CAR I NEED:
I need a four-door family car. I would love a truck or a luxury car, but the latter is way expensive and the former would only be used occasionally.

List of Options Wanted:

FEATURE	SELECTION
Air conditioning	yes/no
Anti-lock brakes	yes/no
Anti-theft package	yes/no
Color	_____
Cruise control	yes/no
Doors (number)	2/3/4/5
Extended warranty	yes/no
Exterior protection packages	yes/no
Interior package	yes/no
Interior protection packages	yes/no
Life insurance	yes/no
Light package	yes/no
Motor size (number of cylinders)	4/6/8/12
Power features:	
◆ power seats	yes/no
◆ power mirrors	yes/no
◆ power windows	yes/no
◆ power doors	yes/no
Roof rack	yes/no
Rust protection	yes/no

Safety features: air bag, etc.	yes/no
Sound system (buy elsewhere?)	yes/no
Special features:	
◆ center console	yes/no
◆ other _____	yes/no
Suspension type	_____
Tilt wheel	yes/no
Top styles:	
◆ T-top	yes/no
◆ moon roof	yes/no
◆ convertible	yes/no
◆ hard top	yes/no
Towing package	yes/no
Transmission type	automatic/manual
Trim packages:	
◆ including special upholstery	yes/no
◆ exterior trim	yes/no
◆ leather	yes/no
◆ pockets	yes/no
◆ drink holders	yes/no
◆ other _____	yes/no
Type of seats	bench/bucket
Other specials _____	yes/no

(such as a still higher level sound system, CD players, etc.)

Some of these options come only in a package that includes a number of items sold together. For instance, you may not be able to get air conditioning without a package that includes power steering, power door locks, cruise control, and a tilt steering wheel. There is usually no flexibility in these packages.

Now that you have decided what the car will be used for, what type of car you need, and what options are essential to you, you can concentrate your homework effort on assessing the performance and availability of your choice and its options. The key element here is to find the areas of the car's performance that are critical to you and to rate the car accordingly. For instance, a person who needs a performance car and who trades in a car every year or two may be less interested in reliability than in acceleration and style. Likewise, someone who buys a family car and holds it for ten years is likely to be more interested in usable back seats and reliability than in styling. Therefore see how the experts rate your car and see how their recommendations suit your situation.

Ratings by experts can be obtained from car magazines such as *Road and Track* or *Car and Driver* or other publications such as *Consumer Reports* and specialty books like those mentioned earlier. It also would be useful to talk to friends, relatives, neighbors, etc., who have purchased cars similar to those you are considering.

On a scale of 1 (least) to 10 (most), rate the following items for your needs. Then see how the vehicle you are considering fits this profile as rated by the experts in the car magazines.

Priority Rating Charts

CHARACTERISTIC	MY PRIORITIES	RATING BY EXPERTS
acceleration		
braking		
bumpers		
controls		
cost		
displays		
driving position		
emergency handling		
front seating		
fun to drive		
gas mileage		
heating		
noise		
rear seating		
reliability		
ride		
routine handling		
servicing		
towing capability		
trunk		
value		
ventilation		

Special Items Wanted:

ITEM	WANTED	RATING BY EXPERTS
air conditioning	yes/no	
cruise control	yes/no	
luxury package	yes/no	
moon roof	yes/no	

power brakes	yes/no	_____
power steering	yes/no	_____
roof rack	yes/no	_____
special engine	yes/no	_____
special exterior package	yes/no	_____
special interior package	yes/no	_____
special suspension	yes/no	_____
special tires	yes/no	_____
T-top	yes/no	_____
tilt steering	yes/no	_____
towing package	yes/no	_____
other_____	yes/no	_____
other_____	yes/no	_____
other_____	yes/no	_____

Special Recommendations of Experts

upgrade engine	yes/no
upgrade suspension	yes/no
upgrade transmission	yes/no
automatic or stick	_____
preferred model	_____
corporate twin available	yes/no
other_____	yes/no
other_____	yes/no

- Is the vehicle a first-year design of uncertain reliability?   yes/no
- Do the experts say this is important?   yes/no
- Do the experts think the styling is dated?   yes/no
- Is this the last year the car will be produced? (like a Merkur or a Renault)   yes/no
- Is the vehicle in great demand?   yes/no

Final List

Now look over all the data you have gathered and list the cars (company and model) that fill the bill.

1. _____
2. _____
3. _____
4. _____

CALCULATING AFFORDABILITY

This section is designed to help you calculate how much you can afford to pay for a car.

1. Maximum *total* price you can afford to pay $_____

    (You can either put in a number here, or you can take the maximum monthly payments you can afford times the number of months you want to pay to get the maximum amount you can afford to pay for the vehicle. For example $300 a month for 60 months = $18,000. Make this a realistic figure and use it as a guide above which you will not go, even under pressure.)

2. Maximum monthly payment you can afford $_____

    (Note: Do not tell these numbers to the salesperson because if you say, "I can only afford $325/month," he will feel that you can afford at least $350/month and probably more.)

3. Realistic price for a suitable type vehicle $_____
    (You can get this from your literature search)

4. What is your trade-in worth? $_____
    (Get this from your Blue Book wholesale less $200-400)

5. How much cash can you put down? $_____

6. Taxes, licenses, and other fees $_____

7. Transportation cost $_____

8. Extended warranty and other extras $_____

9. Factory rebates $_____

    (Factory-to-consumer or a piece of the factory-to-dealer rebates)

10. Premiums, an AMU or an ADMU $_____
    (additional dealer markup, or extra profit)

11. Options, extras, special tires, etc. $_____

Total to be Financed:

$3 + 6 + 7 + 8 + 10 + 11 - 4 - 5 - 9 =$ $_____

   This calculation will give you a good approximation of the car's actual price. Many times, people forget item #6, the costs of the taxes, licenses, and fees. In California in 1992, the sales tax ran as high as 8.5%, the registration fee as much as 2%, and extra small fees such as a document fee or a luxury tax could boost the price of item #6 to over 10% of the final cost of the vehicle. This is a major item. If you don't know the tax and fee situation in your area, contact your local Division of Motor Vehicles or any local dealer.

Experiment with your calculation. For instance, substitute various values of your trade-in. Take Blue Book wholesale, or auction price, or Blue Book wholesale less $300 and see how this affects the total amount to be financed. For #9 see if the car becomes much more affordable if Detroit gives a factory to consumer rebate of $1000 on your vehicle.

Sample Financial Calculation:

1.	Maximum *total* price you can afford to pay	$15,600.00
2.	Maximum monthly payment you can afford	$325.00
3.	Realistic price for a suitable type vehicle	$18,000.00
4.	What is your trade-in worth?	$7,100.00
5.	How much cash can you put down?	$2,736.00
6.	Taxes, licenses, and other fees	$1,790.00
7.	Transportation cost	$475.00
8.	Extended warranty and other extras	$1,250.00
9.	Factory rebates	$750.00
10.	Premiums, an AMU or an ADMU	$0.00
	(This should *always* be $0.00. This reminds you that you did not pay this extra amount for the vehicle)	
11.	Options, extras, special tires, etc.	$500.00

Total to be Financed:

18,000 + 1790 + 475 + 1250 + 0 + 500 - 7100 - 2736 - 750 = $11,429.00

Amount of Money Available to Spend on a Car

1.	Expressed as total dollars	$_____
2.	Expressed as monthly payments	$_____

This gives you the dollar amount to be financed. For an accurate monthly payment go to a book of interest amortization tables and figure out what your monthly payments would be. For the example above we'll round down the amount to be financed to $11,000.00

interest of	14.5%
and a term of	48 months
you would expect monthly payments of	$303.36
which would be a total payment of	$14,561.28
or interest of	$3,561.28

So it looks like you can stay within your $325/month limit and afford about an $18,000 car if your figures are even approximately correct.

Now that you know how much money you can afford to pay for your car, find out what cars fall into that price range. (One word of caution, don't let the salesperson do this type of "what kind of car can I afford?"

calculation for you. He will try to confuse you and convince you to get a more expensive car than you really want.)

Now with your decision made, your research done, and your financial calculations in front of you, you are ready to make a choice. You can easily decide if you can afford the new car you want.

One other item of homework to consider: There are two types of rebates, *Factory to Customer* and *Factory to Dealer*. It would be very useful to obtain information about what type of rebates are given from the Factory to the Dealers. You will know about Factory to Customer rebates because they are widely advertised and automatically presented by the dealer to the customer. Not so for *Factory to Dealer* rebates, they are hidden. These rebates come and go. If you get an anomalously low price on your new dream car, this may be a reason for it—a rebate you didn't know existed.

This is a number I found in the latest *Edmund's New Car Prices for 1993* (Edmund's Publications Corp., 1993) on page 229. *Edmund's* gives the phone number of Nationwide Auto Brokers, Inc. and they will give you the most current information on incentives and rebates. The number is (313)559-6661.

Best Choice:

Make it, write it down, and never look back.

Now that you know yourself, your needs, and what your budget will bear, it's time to strategize on how to get the money you need to purchase your car.

Getting Loans

Most car buyers don't have the money to make cash auto transactions. Ninety percent of all car buyers must finance their purchases. Usually they try their bank loan officer first, so it becomes important to understand the banking industry's auto loan process.

BANKS AND THEIR FUNCTION

Bankers in their habitat are a strange breed, and I make no claims to understanding them. Loan officers are usually underpaid. Although banks are high on prestige, they are low on salary. However, these same loan officers seem to control our ability to purchase the vehicle we want. We need them in order to get money at lower rates than those available from a dealership, to afford to buy a better car. If you wait until you sell your old car, buy a new car, and get all the extras you want to try to obtain reasonable financing, you may be in for a shock. It is always better to get your money first, then go after the car. This section is going to show you how best to get that loan money.

Let's look at banks and loan officers and see what they are and what they want.

First, the institutions themselves are very conscious of security and of making sure that the loans are repaid, that they are repaid profitably, and that no one skips out with the bank's vehicle before the loan is paid off.

Second, they want to make loans. Really they do! It's how they make money. If they only took in deposits and did not invest what they received in houses, cars, and other things, they would make no money and would quickly go broke.

The combination of the first and second points is enough to make them schizophrenic. They think, "We will loan you *our* money because we must in order to survive, but *you* must treat it right, and give it back to us at regular intervals. You must not make us nervous, because we want to be safe, and the only way we can feel safe is not to lend to people who make us nervous."

Third, banks structure their sales staff (loan officers and behind-the-scenes people who spend all day in offices approving loan applications on essentially a salary basis). These people receive no benefits other than pats on the back for making more loans. They do not receive monetary incentives. They are not highly commissioned like vinyl siding sales-people and thus tend to judge loans by the consumer loan application. Although bankers get no commissions for making profitable loans, if the loan goes bad they have explaining to do. If a large number of their loans go bad, they have a lot of explaining to do. They might even lose their jobs. If they make a mistake, it is going to be on the conservative, "I won't loan you that money" side.

Fourth, the people who make the decision about the loan never see the loan consumer. The impression you make with the bank officer is somewhat muted by the fact that this is not the person who approves the loan. However, if you do not make a good impression on the loan officer, you won't ever make it to the approval headquarters.

HOW LOANS ARE PROCESSED

1. The bank loan officer talks to the customer, pre-qualifies him, helps him fill out the application, and then ships it back to head-quarters for approval.
2. The headquarters people approve or deny the loan based on the application and on their own internal factors and ship the results back to the bank loan officer. The application is important, because the person who does the loan will not see the customer or know how nice he is, and will only go by some hard monetary facts and his credit history.
3. The branch bank loan officer can, within certain limits, overrule a central bank denial of an application. This override ability seems to fluctuate with the economy and is not a common occurence. But the fact that it is possible should stress the importance of favorably impressing your banker.
4. Bankers have assured me that while loans can be processed on an emergency basis in eight hours, routine approvals are done in two to three days. If your bank tells you that it will take three to four weeks, ask them why and either check another bank or threaten to do so.
5. For new car loans, many California banks currently (early 1993) are lending 80% of selling price for new vehicles and are lending up to

100% of wholesale Blue Book for used vehicles. Obviously, this is subject to change depending on economic conditions. The right bank may even loan for tax and license for used vehicles as well. This goes to show you how much better a bank feels a used car purchase is than a new car purchase.

You may be an inventive and imaginative person. I may be a person who evaluates people and things uniquely: bankers are not like that. They are paid to evaluate things only on a conservative, conventional, and financial basis. How do they evaluate a vehicle conventionally and financially? They base the loan on the price of the new/used vehicle as defined by the manufacturer (list price), the selling agency (dealership), or a recognized used car expert (Blue Book).

This can create problems. For example, for a used car, Blue Book is only an estimate. The Blue Book and others like it cannot hope to show all the factors that can influence a car's price. These factors include regional preferences, seasonal differences, the effect of paint color, interior condition, etc.

In its introduction, the Blue Book says, "Wholesale values are based on clean vehicles fully reconditioned and ready for resale with acceptable mileage as indicated by zeros on the mileage chart." It defines suggested retail values "as an estimated dealer asking price. The actual selling price may vary substantially." It also indicates that, "Condition is of prime importance! Appropriate amounts should be added for exceptionally clean vehicles and vehicles which are under warranty by the factory or the dealer. Appropriate amounts should be deducted for needed reconditioning."

How do banks do this? Do the bankers come out of their air-conditioned offices and go over the vehicles they are going to loan on? Do they check the oil and listen to the engine run? The answer is obviously, "No."

I have taken purchase orders (the documents that dealers give to banks to inform them what is on a car), a VIN (Vehicle Identification Number), and other useful data and gone to a bank. On a hot day, the loan officer didn't want to go out to see the vehicle, and wouldn't even bother to take a look out the window to see if it was a 3/4 ton truck or a VW bus.

Some other bank officers with whom I have worked are so inexperienced that when I took one to see the car in question, she didn't know where the VIN was located, what items on the car to compare to the purchase order, or anything. If she was protecting the bank's investment, that bank was in trouble.

The bank officers compare Blue Book values to what is reported on the purchase order. They seem not to care about the condition of the vehicle or any of the really practical stuff. Yet we all know that color, condition, options, smell, rips in the upholstery, or cigarette burns in the carpeting can drastically affect the desirability of the vehicle and therefore its price.

How can a set of values for a car, which does not cover all the really important items, affect the loan value, which is a measure of the worth of the car? There is no other way to evaluate what a car is worth, or really what the car will be worth if you don't make payments and they have to repossess the vehicle and sell it to get their money back. You then come back to the major value that determines a loan — how the bank can get its money back if it must. If your ability to pay back were so solid as to be absolute, banks would lend you whatever you wanted on your vehicle, even if you grossly overpaid the dealership.

Therefore, as a borrower, your job is to make yourself appear so solid on a loan application that you can get the best terms possible, both in rate and in percentage of the value of the car. How do you do this?

1. You must look like a good loan candidate. It always helps to dress up, look solid and financially conservative. My banker says the way you look doesn't matter because the loan approval officers are in the central headquarters of the bank and they never see you. Yet, he also indicates that he has the power to overrule a negative loan recommendation if he feels strongly that the loan is viable. What does he base his opinion on? I will bet that it is partially on his personal evaluation based on your meeting with him. A large part of this evaluation will be based on your behavior and dress.

2. Never mention troubles such as divorce or lay-offs. The loan officer will wonder if you will still be able to pay off the car loan with the other demand on your money. Make it look like as much of your income as possible will be available to go towards the loan.

3. Make it look as though there are fewer people enjoying a piece of your income. If you have kids and an ex who get a piece of your pie, your significant other has kids and an ex who get a piece of that pie, and the two of you have kids together, the bank is going to be aware of the constraints on your salary. Of course, the bank will consider your income with deductions, but they will also consider you, your whole tribe, and all your financial obligations and then look at whatever remains as available for repayment of a loan. You get no points for being a good parent.

4. It is best not to even try to receive an out-of-state loan. It has to be a nightmare to repossess an out-of-state car so the loan process is nearly impossible.

5. Do your best to show long, steady work history based on salary and not commissions. Banks object to commissions as a basis for a loan because they fluctuate with the economy.

6. Show long-term stability in your residence. Banks like to know where to go if it is ever necessary to repossess their vehicles.

7. If you feel your loan history may be marginal, and most of us know that our credit history will have some flaws, it may be good to get a copy of your credit history (TRW) and look at it before the loan interview. You can get to see your TRW credit report by calling (800) 392-1122. This will allow you to be ready to answer questions about any questionable items (any late payments or disputes).

8. A lot of people are embarrassed about their credit history and feel that banks are so respectable and upscale that they will not go to them and risk embarrassment. They would rather go to an auto dealership, pay more, and avoid the discomfort and anxiety, even though most dealerships ultimately finance through banks. What you don't want to do is to worry about your credit to the point that you do not go to a bank, but go to a dealership and "throw yourself at their mercy."

9. Make sure you ask for enough money to be able to get what you need and want. Don't "starve" yourself; make sure that you borrow enough money for the vehicle that you want.

WRAP-UP

Go to a bank or credit union armed with a preview of your own TRW credit report. Argue for the best rates available, and come out of the bank with a loan in *advance* of your trip to a dealership. This will enable you to go through an automobile transaction without worrying about how you are going to pay for the car.

It is very important when going for a loan on a new or used car that you *make sure the bank knows who you are buying a car from.* Let them know if you are buying from a dealer, from a private party, or at auction. This will prevent the bank canceling the loan based on a misunderstanding.

Now that you know how to secure an auto loan from a bank, you are ready for the next part of your homework: how to find out what your used car is really worth.

4

Your Trade-In

As specified in Chapter 6, the first step when negotiating with the sales-person is determining your trade-in price. This initial step is the most difficult one for some people because their car is a part of them and selling it is a very emotional issue. Buying a car is hard, selling your present car is even harder. In order to get the best price for your trade-in, you have to know what it is really worth to the dealer. He won't give you more for it than it is worth, but he will certainly try to give you a lot less.

Everybody knows you really love your used car, and everybody knows that it got you through the snowstorm of '88 and through the flood of '78 and it was the best of the litter in '68. But you must evaluate your car realistically, as a potential buyer would. Someone who just needs transportation, nothing more, does not regard rusted-through holes as increased ventilation.

Here's how to check to see what your vehicle is really worth, so that when you try to get maximum dollar for it, you are trying for a realistic figure.

Check the Blue Book (use a local bank or library) and evaluate the worth of the car. Include considerations for mileage and for extra features (or damage). Find a copy machine and copy both the base page and the mileage page for your records and calculations. Banks will be glad to give you this information and to show you how to read the figures. Tell them you want to buy a car and are considering using them for the financing. Make sure that you receive a current reference book, not one that is months or even years old.

$_____ Blue Book wholesale value
$_____ estimated value of options (+ or -)
$_____ estimated value of mileage (+ or -)

$_____ total wholesale value of car (base + options + mileage)

$_____   Blue Book base "retail" value
$_____   estimated value of options (+ or -)
$_____   estimated value of mileage (+ or -)

$_____   total retail value of car (base + options + mileage)

You may find that different evaluations may not come out the same. That is to be expected as these evaluations are approximate. The evaluations do not take into account a variety of factors including condition, color, and whether the car is currently "hot." Also, the Blue Book does not always reflect market changes in the value of a vehicle. For instance, Audi was a highly regarded upscale automobile. Then *Consumer Reports* published an article on unintended acceleration. This destroyed Audi's reputation in the United States. The actual street value of an Audi deviated wildly from the previously published wholesale values.

Remember, the Blue Book and others try to follow and report the market, not predict it. Naturally, they will deviate strongly from it in some circumstances. Use the Blue Book as a first look at a vehicle's worth. It is great for that.

Read the newspapers and see what price people are asking for vehicles of this type. Usually the asking price will fall somewhere between low Blue Book (wholesale) and high Blue Book (retail).

$_____   First Newspaper Price
$_____   Second Newspaper Price
$_____   Third Newspaper Price

Don't be shy. Respond to some ads for vehicles similar to yours and see what kind of action the sellers are getting. Also get any facts they are willing to share. Most people are so anxious to sell their cars they share information easily. If their vehicle does not have an automatic transmission, ask them if it has been a barrier to the sale. If the car is fully loaded, ask if that has helped the sale even though it raised the price. If they have sold their vehicle, get the figures and see how it relates to your vehicle. The prices they quote will be very useful in determining how high a price you can expect to get from a dealership. If people selling vehicles similar to your trade-in on the street are getting very good prices, perhaps you should try selling it yourself. Street prices do reflect the retail market: you may be surprised at the low price the dealerships will first offer for your trade-in. Remember, they are selling to the same retail market and should be able to pay more for the car since they can sell it for a profit even though they have to fix it up and guarantee it.

Check with some used car dealers and see what they want for a car of this type. What would they buy or sell it for? Check the market. Is your car hot or cold, a seller or a sitter? If it is a hot seller, be firm on the price you want from a dealership. If it is not moving, you may have to drop considerably below Blue Book wholesale to sell it.

$_____ Dealer's Buy Price
$_____ Dealer's Sell Price

If you have the contacts, see what your car would sell for at a dealers only auction. See if someone will sell it there for you for a small commission. You may come out ahead if you do it that way.

The auction price of a vehicle at a dealers only auction is interesting. If a dealership takes in a car as a trade-in, it may decide that it doesn't want to retail this particular car itself. The reasons for this vary, but may have nothing to do with the car's condition. Dealers only auctions provide a marketplace where vehicles can be bought and sold quickly. Auction advantages are the possibility of a quick sale at a reasonable price. Therefore, if a dealership "steals a car" from a customer at $2200, it may sell it at auction for say $2950, and pocket the $750 (minus expenses). If a dealership can't get a car below auction prices it may not buy the trade-in, but may buy a similar car at auction and save money.

$_____ Auction Price

DEALER QUOTES

Auto dealers will try to *lowball* you and tell you that they can't even give you Blue Book wholesale for your vehicle. They will say that now everybody gives only auction prices for a used car. They will then quote you a much lower price than auction prices. For instance, if Blue Book retail is $5900 and Blue Book wholesale is $4500 and a typical auction price is $4100, they will offer you $2900 for your car and may go as high as $3200 if pressed.

Dealerships believe they can get away with this and often they do. This is true for a number of reasons:

1. Most people don't know what their car is worth. The usual initial reaction is that the car is worth a lot. When pressed, car owners just give the vehicles away with a whine and a whimper because they don't really know how high a price is realistic.
2. Most people are either embarrassed by negotiating or don't know how to fight for a better price. This discomfort is exacerbated if the other party is strong-willed, seems knowledgeable, and is intentionally intimidating. They feel they have only two choices when

presented with a deal, *take it* or *leave it*. They rarely negotiate for price or conditions. They are basically ignorant of the value of a vehicle even though they are sure the dealer is giving them a very low price for their trade-in. People generally give in if anything resembling a reasonable explanation for the low offer is presented to them.

3. Salespeople are experienced negotiators and leave themselves some maneuvering room so they can later raise the price if they must. Who knows, the customer may just take the lowball offer or the dealership may not have to raise the offer very much. When a customer hears a salesperson say, "I will give you $1850 for your Buick," what the salesperson is really saying is, "My *initial* offer for your vehicle is *at least* $1850 and is probably *more*."

    What the customer thinks is, "I either have to accept his $1850 or walk out and not get a new car here." Since the customer really wants a new car, she is not likely to refuse the $1850.

    In reality, this is only the opening gambit in a negotiating scene. The salesperson is just fishing to see what will be accepted. He is hoping that this first price is taken. But remember, it is just his first move in a bidding cycle. It is certainly not a take it or leave it situation. As soon as you begin to understand his offer as just that, an offer, it will be easier for you to counter rather than feel pressured to "take it or leave it."

4. Who knows, maybe the customer won't argue at all. She might not care and more than likely just wants to get this unpleasant task over with. It is worth a try just to see. If the customer accepts a lowball for $1000 less than her vehicle is worth because she really doesn't want to argue, the dealership can make $1000 in just a few seconds. That is pretty good pay in these troubled economic times.

5. Dealerships don't have problems financing customers if they make their profit with a low price for the trade-in. Banks have rules about financing. The main concern of a bank is not financing a customer as a public service, but insuring that if the customer defaults on the loan, the bank can retrieve its investment. How do they do this? By loaning less than 100% of the car's value. If the dealership makes its money by selling a car at list or — heaven forbid — above list, the bank may be reluctant to lend all that extra profit. If the car has to be repossessed and sold, it will not return enough money to satisfy the bank's investment. So what better way to make your profit than to get it on the non-financed portion of the car deal; the trade-in.

6. People usually buy their new car first and *then* determine what their used car can bring. By that time they are so emotionally committed

to their new car they don't even care about getting the best price for their trade-in. They have devalued their old car in their own minds and won't fight hard for a better price for it. This is why it is better to get your price for your trade-in first, before you psychologically feel that the beautiful new car is yours and switch allegiance from the old vehicle to the new one.

7. Many people are unable to sell their cars themselves, so they have no choice but to accept the dealer's prices. This is a tough situation to be in. The customer needs a new car and wants to get rid of her trade-in. She is not comfortable selling it herself and for the same reasons is not comfortable negotiating with a dealership for a better trade-in price. What does she usually do? She just gives in and gets the trade-in negotiation over with.

Remember to try for Blue Book wholesale for your trade-in, but be prepared to settle for something less. If you can get wholesale, congratulations. Never settle for less than auction price; you can *always* get that. A *good* price through a dealership would be wholesale minus $300. If you are unable to get that and feel comfortable doing so, try to sell the car yourself.

NEGOTIATE

Remember, always negotiate trade-in price *before* you negotiate new car price.

$_____   Dealer's first offer on your used car

$_____   Dealer's next offer on your used car

$_____   Dealer's best offer on your used car

$_____   How does it compare to wholesale?

$_____   auction?

$_____   retail?

It is very important that you get the very best price for your trade-in. One of the best ways to do this is to repeat the following points.

First, tell the dealer that it is *very important* that you get the very best price for your trade-in and that after you get your price for the trade-in, the rest of the sale will go easily. Sales staff look at each customer to see what is important to him or her. If the trade-in price is important, the dealership will give it to them *if* the salesperson feels that the rest of the deal will go down easily. The salesperson needs to feel sure that the necessary profit can be picked up in other areas of the transaction, such as on the new car price.

Second, tell the salesperson that you need a good trade-in price for your car in order to afford a down payment. This is a great reason. Even if it is not relevant in your case, it is a great reason. Many people have good jobs, but live right to the limit of their incomes. They can make payments of $200, $300, or more, but find it tough to come up with $3600 in cash. The best way for them to raise cash for a down payment is to get a good price for their trade-in to apply to the down payment, thereby keeping the cash portion of the down payment low. Lead the salesperson to believe that this is your situation.

After you have been promised an acceptable price for your trade-in, you can stress the importance of other elements of the transaction. Initially, the only important thing is getting a good price for your trade-in. Later, when the salesperson tries to get a higher price for the new car, take the position that the only thing important to you is a good price on the new car. The salesperson is trapped at that point, having already agreed to a good price on the trade-in. He has already invested a considerable amount of time on you and does not want to risk losing the sale at this point.

When you've settled the trade-in issue and have a firm commitment from the dealer on a price, your mind is free to decide on a realistic price for the new car. How well you can do this determines how well you and your pocketbook will fare in the important second phase of the car buy, getting that new car.

5

Going to the Showroom

Now that you have researched the realistic worth of your trade-in, you are *almost* ready to step foot in that pressure chamber: the showroom. Let's see what else it makes sense to bring with you to help you buy that car. This chapter will cover what to bring, how to dress to look like a real customer, and what kind of an attitude to have to convince the sales force that you are a person to be reckoned with. You have done all your homework and have that information at your fingertips; now you are ready to visit the showroom.

WHAT AND WHOM TO BRING

A Distractor

It is always a good idea to bring someone who can help you. If you are inexperienced and/or have a gentle personality, bring a strong spouse or someone else who will pull you out of the fire if necessary.

Let me tell you why it is desirable to bring along a distractor, or "a third baseman," as he/she is called. From your normal, everyday experiences, it seems that you would want to have your hands on all the power and be able to do whatever is necessary to ensure closing the deal. In fact, my experience has shown me that it is actually better not to have the power to make the final decision when you enter into a car negotiation. It is still better to have someone with you whose only job is to make sure that things *don't* happen according to the plan of the sales staff. Car salespeople, as we shall see in a later chapter, work on the theory of limited authority. From his position of limited authority, the salesperson verbally agrees to any kind of deal you want. He does this in order to find out what you can really afford. Later, he claims not to have the authority to finalize the deal. Then his manager reworks the arrangement and demands more money from you.

Each time you have to negotiate with a manager or new salesperson, you start from a more vulnerable position and in the process give up more. It works to your advantage if the salesperson feels that you can't make the final decision. It is also very helpful to have someone with you to distract the salesperson and relieve the pressure when "teams" of experienced sales staff start pushing you to make decisions.

The following exchange is a good illustration.

SALESPERSON (closing in for the "kill"): Now that we have answered all your objections, what will it take to get you to buy this car today, right now? (This is known as the "California approach.")

YOU (feeling a lot of pressure): Well, the car is nice and I really can't think of a reason not to buy it now, but … (You are now getting ready to give away the store.)

THIRD BASEMAN (giving you time to think): Excuse me, but does this car come in yellow? I really like yellow.

SALESPERSON (really irritated that his "close" has been interrupted and the mood broken, but unwilling to attack the idiot who is with the buyer because he looks like the buyer's best friend): No, it doesn't. Now, as I was asking, what do you want to pay for this great car that we have spent the last three hours looking at?

THIRD BASEMAN (still giving you time to think): Why not? It would look great in yellow.

SALESPERSON (ignoring the third baseman): Why don't you just give me a bid to take to my manager and then we can see if he accepts it.

YOU: Why *doesn't* it come in yellow?

SALESPERSON (frustrated but unwilling to offend a "real" buyer): The manufacturer makes that car in only four colors with four matching upholsteries.

YOU: (Having had time to think and to resist the pressures of the salesperson): Let's talk a little bit more about getting a better price for my trade-in. As you know, the trade-in price is very important to me in terms of my ability to make a good down payment.

In this example, the pressure position has passed and you can go on with your bid to buy a car. Often, the sales staff are very practiced in their presentation. Interruptions of this sort take them off-guard, and it is not easy for them to find their way back to the practiced flow of their high-pressure pitch.

A Yellow Pad and Two Types of Pens

These are necessary so that you can write notes with a fine tip and write big agreement items (like trade-in price) with a big magic marker so that the salesperson will see them. Anything written down has more significance than the spoken word. Verbal "agreements" can later be misinterpreted or forgotten. An agreed upon price or figure carries a lot more weight if it is put into print. If the salesperson has a casual attitude toward his claims and prices has a talent for making figures appear and disappear at will, writing down the figures makes his utterance more permanent. If he then gives you a variety of prices for your trade-in, you can quote — and point to — the highest when it is suitable. If you feel comfortable, show the numbers to him as you go along, ask for a verbal confirmation, and ask him to initial the figures. His initialing of the figures does not bind him to them, as he is operating from his position of limited authority, but it *does* force him to stick with that figure in your discussions. This prevents him from confusing you by throwing around numbers at will.

The Results of Your Homework

Keep your homework results out of sight until needed. I went on a car buy with a young woman (maybe twenty-two or twenty-three). Prior to going to the dealership, we had worked out the prices we would accept for her trade-in and for her new car. We wrote down the figures so that we could remember them and refer to them during the appropriate time in the negotiations. She put those figures on the bottom of her notebook. After the test drive, she held her books and papers to her chest — facing out — as we were talking to the sales staff outside the negotiating room. The figures were exposed, giving the salesperson a pretty good idea of where we were going to end up.

We were still able to get close to our prices for the deal because they made sense. The economics of the situation still determined what could happen. We had allowed for the dealership to make some money — although less than they would have preferred.

Remember, do the preliminary library work and the figuring and keep the figures handy, but out of sight.

Reference Books and Papers

Treat reference books and papers just as you do like your homework. Keep the books handy, but out of sight.

Calculator

Use your calculator whenever the salesperson is working with figures. Don't blindly accept what is told to you. Do the figuring for the salesperson if you can. Use the calculator to do the figuring; it makes you more active and the salesperson more passive. It also takes away his ability to confuse you with inaccurate figures. He may still try to finagle the whole system of numbers, but it is more difficult if you are doing the math. Be careful not to let the busywork of doing the calculations pull your attention away from your main job — getting the best deal. It is a common tactic for salespeople to give interested buyers something to do so that they are not thinking about whether or not the deal is a good one.

Interest and Payment Tables

At the end of the buy, after the trade-in has been worked out, the new car price agreed upon, and the financing arrangements determined, pull out your interest and payment tables and double-check the figures presented to you. It gives one a great feeling of confidence to be able to check the dealer's calculations of monthly payments. It increases your level of confidence in the negotiations. You are assured that the figures given you for the payments are accurate. The finance person knows that if she tries to change the numbers at the end, you will catch the changes.

Payment or Financing Verification from Your Lender

As we discussed earlier in the homework section, it is to your advantage to provide your own financing. If you have obtained your own financing, have all the paperwork handy and ready to show at the appropriate time. You lose a lot of negotiating power if you have to promise to return the next day with loan confirmation. Have all of this completed *before* you visit the salesroom. If you come into the dealership with an approved low interest loan, you can probably get them to reduce their rates.

Proof of Insurance

In many places, you must have insurance to drive. Make sure that you have the details of your auto insurance handy. An insurance card will do nicely.

If you have a trade-in there are a number of other details you should have in order. These are:

A Clean Car

I am always amazed that people who take good care of their homes or clean up articles for a garage sale, do not take the same care in presenting their cars to a dealership as potential trade-ins. A potential trade-in should be as well detailed as possible, immaculately clean, and have all personal papers removed. Repair records and items pertinent to the sale of the trade-in vehicle should be left in the glove compartment. Nothing else should be in the car.

When dealerships put a car out for sale in their lots, they "detail" the inside and outside of a vehicle, and in many cases steam clean the engine to make it show better to customers. If the dealership is your customer for the trade-in, should you do any less to secure a good price? Your intention should be to leave your old car at the dealership and to drive away in a new car. It is important that it be ready for them to put on the lot "as is." This will increase your bargaining power on a price for the trade-in.

Documentation of Debt

If you owe money on your vehicle, get documentation showing the exact amount of money left to be paid off. If you have your vehicle paid off, bring verification of this. This can be found on the title; the lien holder had to sign off once the debt to him was fulfilled.

All of the Keys to Your Car

Give one set of keys to the dealership's used car evaluator, but keep one set with you until the transaction is complete. This way if the deal goes sour, you can still drive off in your trade-in and not be held hostage by the dealership. Yes, they do it if they can.

The Title for Your Trade-in

Bring the title for at least two reasons. First, to show that your car is paid off; and second, to show that the title is a normal title and not some "limited" title like a salvage title. The value of a vehicle can drop dramatically if the car has a salvage title. In states that have salvage titles, they indicate that the car has been "scrapped" (for reasons such as a bad accident) and then rebuilt and the title reactivated. A vehicle with a salvage title may run well, but its perceived value, and therefore its resale value, is substantially lower.

Service Records

Nothing sells a car like a verifiable history of good service. This is especially important for the more expensive, luxury cars, but is also useful for the less expensive models.

HOW TO DRESS

Wear comfortable, presentable clothes. It is important that you are both comfortable and presentable. You are going to be at the dealership for several hours and it is important that you give the impression of being a real buyer. Tight clothing will make you uncomfortable; ripped or torn clothing will not get you a better price on the car, nor any sympathy — but it may get you a higher interest rate on your financing.

Stay away from low necklines or distracting clothing. You can't be tough if you don't look tough. Keep the issues on the car, not on any other topic. The typical car salesperson may be influenced by style, fashion, or skin exposure, but in most cases it will be business before pleasure.

THE BEST CAR-BUYING ATTITUDE

It is important to enter the showroom with certain attitudes firmly entrenched. Your body language should match your clothing and the thoroughness of your homework. You must be clear in your mind that you will buy a car today *if* the price is right and *if* you are treated well both personally and financially.

Remember that you are the customer. *They* have the car and *they* must sell it. You can live without it for a while longer. Do not allow yourself to feel pressured. Remind yourself that the salesperson is the one who is desperate. Go with the attitude, "Treat me right or I am out of here; I will not be messed with."

Don't be emotional. Be a little unpredictable and cool. If you feel you are being treated badly or not taken seriously, be firm and let them know about it. Remember not to gush about the car. If you do, you will pay more for it. But don't be too negative either. Be neutral.

Don't be afraid to speak up. You must ask for a good deal to get one. Be ready to deal if the price and everything else are right.

Salespeople are trained to determine in the first several minutes exactly what kind of customer you are. Once this is settled in their minds, they choose a game plan to follow in order to "handle" you to their best advantage. It is definitely to your advantage — and very disconcerting for them — for you suddenly to show them that their whole strategy for selling you a car is not working. They have to rethink their strategy at the last minute and it is difficult to change pace and negate all the things they have said previously to make you buy a car.

Play dumb if it helps you. Saying, "Huh?" or "I'm sorry, I just don't understand," will put them off-guard. You don't have to know everything to do well in a negotiation. Don't be too smart at first. It is a better strategy to be a little confused, uncertain, and weak at first and then as the negotiations progress, your true nature can come through, allowing you to completely control the negotiations.

Here is how to get that winning attitude:

♦   Clear your mind of extraneous details. Don't go to a buy with a head full of troubles. Once you enter that showroom, the car buy should be your first and only priority. Get the other items out of the way before you buy. If other items are pressing you and crowding your mind, put them off. If you have no car and need one, rent a car for a few days until you complete any distracting projects.

♦   Know that your financing homework is done and that for all intents and purposes, you have the cash "in hand." This will give you confidence and will prevent you from being held up by later financing problems. I cannot emphasize enough how important it is that you have your financing lined up before you physically start shopping. That way, you will never have to worry if you can get your dream car financing from the dealership. You will never have to take a bad deal in order to get dealer financing: you will have your own.

♦ Limit the negotiations to one car, two at the most. The sales staff will look at you as a browser, if you negotiate in general rather than on one specific car. Negotiating for a particular blue Taurus on the lot right now is very different than negotiating for a family car. In addition, it is hard to do "general" homework of the depth described earlier.

♦ Know what your trade-in is worth, what you can get the new car for, and what options you want. Be prepared. You can wing it, of course, but it will cost you in your wallet.

♦ Remember, it's your money. *You* are the customer. *If* he presents it well, treats you well, and gives you a great deal, you *may* buy his car. Your money can be spent at another dealership, or it can be spent on things unrelated to automobiles. If the dealership wants your money for their car, let them court you and treat you well.

♦ Demand good treatment. A lack of warmth and some reserve will keep a distance between them and you, which is what you want. Most salespeople believe that if you like them, they will have more success making the sale. They will go out of their way to make you like them in order to facilitate closing a deal. Don't give them that edge. Keep them at enough of a distance so that friendship (which really doesn't exist here) does not become a factor.

TOTAL IMAGE

You want to be considered a real buyer. This gives you a lot of latitude in the way you operate and in how much the dealership will tolerate.

Since you want to be treated as a person who will buy a car *today* if treated well, tell them so. Then act and look like it. This is where dress and manner come in. It is easier for the dealer to sell a car to someone who is financially solvent in both dress and manner. Let them see that you have changeable moods and cannot be trifled with. If this is not your basic nature, bring a "third baseman" who can act this way. Try acting this way for a short period of time yourself and see if you can pull it off.

To make a salesperson willing to spend his time with you, including overtime, you have to make him feel that you are a real buyer. How do you do that? Let's review how to make the sales staff view and treat you like a real buyer.

1. Come well dressed (not outlandishly) and look prosperous. Look as though you can afford to buy a car. People usually get better car buys and better financing if they look as if they are well-educated and can afford the vehicle. Interestingly enough, the time in negotiations will decrease if you look prosperous, competent, and do not allow yourself to be tricked.

   Make sure that your clothes are comfortable so that you can stand, sit, yell, and negotiate in them without being embarrassed or uncomfortable.

2. Come with your trade-in clean, empty, and ready to be traded. Have the papers handy and any information about money owed on the car. Come with all the keys. This illustrates that you are the kind of person who will buy a car *today* if everything is right. This is the kind of person for whom car dealers make allowances and the kind of person with whom they will willingly spend a lot of their time.

3. Say the magic words, "I want to buy a car today." Repeat it several times in different ways and make it believable. However, be sure not to say anything about financing, leasing, or monthly payments. *If these three items don't get their attention, nothing will.*

If you are going to look the part you must also act the part. Showing too much interest or gushing over a car will prove to be expensive ultimately. Acting too negatively is counterproductive. The correct attitude is crucial. Here are some reminders about attitude.

♦ Play it cool, be a little flaky and not overly friendly. Be unpredictable, indicate over and over that you want to buy a car *today* and that you can afford the vehicle.

♦ Don't drool on the hood of the car you love. Be neutral and non-committal.

♦ Don't be too negative. This only makes the sales staff defensive. If you are constantly negative, they assume it means a sale is not in the near future. It will not buy you respect, or a cheaper car. It will not make you look like a real buyer.

♦ Go with the proper companion: no kids! Take along only people who will be useful to you in picking the car or in the negotiations.

♦ Be ready to deal if the deal is right. Be a real buyer. This is important. You have gone through all this trouble to get a great deal, don't inch up to the edge of a buy and then back out. Decide before you go out to look at a car if you are ready to buy one or not.

♦ You must ask for a good deal. Don't be so shy that you wait for them to *offer* a good deal. It will never happen.

♦ Tell the salesperson only what he needs to know. He will probe you for information about your job, why you want to buy a car, and your financial situation. He will also want to know if you want to buy or lease. Tell him only what you want him to know when you want him to know it. Everything he learns will be used against you. Consider having a friend give you the following "Miranda Warning" before you go onto a car lot:

Do you understand that you are going to spend a lot of money?
Do you understand that a lot of pressure will be put on you?
Do you realize that every scrap of information you give a salesperson will be used against you?

Remember, the salesperson doesn't care if you love Buffalo or the Forty-Niners, but if you indicate that you have seasons tickets to the Raiders he will become an instant Raiders fan. He may also assume that if you can afford season tickets, you may be interested in a sportier and more expensive car. Striking up a football friendship may make it easier for him to sell it to you.

Even your most casual comments are really important to a good salesperson. A simple question like, "Does this dealership finance at competitive rates?" indicates to him that you are a real buyer because you have already come to the point in your reasoning process to be interested in interest rates. If you talk about leasing, he knows that people who lease usually pay a higher price for the car. He will then try to focus on lease terms rather than car price. If you give the impression of being financially strapped, needing a car, and act very interested in leasing, you will get a very high interest-rate lease, a low price for your trade-in, and a lot of talk about your bad credit report and how lucky you are to have financing at all. The salesperson probably will not deal with car price at all, and you may not even know what the vehicle cost you.

So reveal only what you want the dealer to know; no more, no less. Slant this to your best advantage. This is sometimes difficult to do. When in doubt, say nothing.

◆ Play dumb if it helps you. You don't have to act smart, especially in the early phases of a negotiation. During the meeting of the salesperson and the test drive, when the salesperson is still trying to classify you, give him a different impression. Later, when it is too late for him to change his tactics and attitude, let him realize that you are in control. Don't be afraid to ask questions, and when hit with technical or sales mumbo jumbo you don't understand, saying, "I don't understand" may put him off-guard.

◆ Say, "This deal is just not good enough," but don't tell him why. Let him offer concessions. Force him to guess if it is the price, the trade-in, the type of car, or the competition. If he is scrambling to make a deal, then he may throw in things you never considered to make the deal go down. If pressed by him to explain why the deal isn't good enough, just say "I don't know, it just doesn't seem good enough." Later, ask for a better price or something more specific.

♦ When you are near an agreement, say "No" just one more time and see what happens. You never know; something else might fall from the tree, especially if it is late at night.

♦ When trying to sell your trade-in, tell the salesperson that the only thing standing in the way of a sale is getting a good price for your used car and after that, everything should be downhill. Then when buying the new car, tell him that the most important thing is getting the best price for your new car.

WHAT AND WHOM NOT TO BRING/DO

Now that we have discussed what to bring, how to behave, and what to do, let's look at the process from the other side: let's see what *not* to bring and do.

♦ Do not bring anyone who won't be able to help you. If you need someone to help choose the color or style, send them away to a movie or anywhere *before* the negotiations begin. I have seen people in dealerships negotiating for a car with their young children spread out playing on blankets in the doorway of the negotiating room. How can the parents leave, walk out of the room, or get upset with those kids blocking the door? To save a few dollars on child care, the parents gave up their mobility and locked themselves in a room with a salesperson (something I would hate to do). This will probably result in their loss of several hundred dollars.

♦ If the person who is supplying the money is not going to be helpful in the buy, have him or her do something else during the negotiations. This may be difficult, but if this person is coming along just to see how you are spending the money and will get in *your* way (not the salesperson's), it is in his best interest not to be there.

♦ Don't put a time limit on yourself — you need the freedom to wait them out or to walk out without encumbrances. If you have to buy a car in order to get to work before 4:00 P.M., you will give away the store to get out of there by 3:30. The salesperson will feel your deadline and will stall until you panic and close the deal in his favor. The best strategy — much more on this later — is to put the dealership under the time limit. Do your buying late in the evening, when the sales force wants to go home.

♦ Don't bring any sort of fear or apprehension. If you have done your homework, you have no reason to be anxious. You will feel more than ready for whatever happens.

6

Order of Operations

You may now feel ready to walk through the door of the dealership, but you still lack one important item: a well thought out plan or strategy to guide you through the complexities of the car-buying process.

It is one thing to read a book on "how to buy a car." It is another thing to be able to utilize the information well in a live vehicle buy. In order to translate research into buying success, you need a system to follow, and that is what this book is about, the development of a winning system. The average, intelligent, untrained amateur should master and depend upon the use of a well thought out, well defined buying strategy.

Obviously, if you are only buying one car every five years, you can't expect to be the best or most proficient at all aspects of car buying—even after reading this book. If you follow the suggestions in this book, especially the order outlined in this chapter, you will undoubtedly get a better deal on your next car purchase.

Remember, as a buyer, you have many strengths. Take advantage of all these and do not be squeamish about using them. Don't feel sorry for the dealership or the sales staff, and don't feel that you have to play by the dealership's rules or follow their agenda. Do what you have to do to control all parts of the car purchase. Most important, *you must execute the various car-buying operations in the right order*. If you do "first things first," you will not be confused or influenced by the tactics a sales force uses to control the buying situation. As a result, you will save more money and they will make less profit.

The only way to know if you are really in control is to make sure that every step gets done correctly, in order, and leads you closer to your new car. You should know *exactly* how much you got paid for your trade-in and how close this price is to Blue Book wholesale. You should know what your new car cost the dealership and exactly how much profit they are making. You should know exactly what factory-to-consumer cash is available to you and what factory-to-dealer incentives are available to the dealer. If you know these figures, then you will know if you are getting a good deal at every step of the transaction. (Factory-to-consumer cash is money paid directly to you, the purchaser of a new car, by the manufacturer. Factory-to-dealer incentives are cash incentives to the dealer that *may* be passed on to you in the form of a lower price.

Finally, the average buyer must know what a good deal is and must be satisfied with it. How do you know what a good deal is? By studying costs and knowing what amounts of profits to allow the dealership. The alternative is to keep grinding away on price, not knowing if what you are asking for is realistic or not.

The key to being able to negotiate is to watch all the costs, not just the price of the new car. A dealer can practically give away the new car and still make plenty of money by "handling you well" on other issues like trade-in's, interest rates, extended warranties, and other options.

The driving force for the dealerships is profits. That means making money on the *total* of the various parts of the negotiation. If they only break even or even lose money on one part, they will make it up on others. Let's look at the parts of a car purchase and examine the order and logic of each.

THE FOUR BASIC PARTS OF AN AUTO BUY

There are four basic parts of a car buy where money can change hands, and all of them must be controlled. These parts, in order, are (1) the used car trade-in, (2) the new car price, (3) buying special packages/options/extras, and (4) financing. Most people focus only on one part, the new car price, and neglect the others. Let's look at these four parts in their preferred order.

The best way to control the negotiations is to operate in the following order. *Do not deviate from this order.* Don't go on to point two before settling on the first point. Don't settle for allowances and always know the *dollar value* of each point. Allowances lose you money.

The Used Car Trade-In

The dealership wants to make a profit on the used car portion of the transaction even if they don't plan on selling your car from their lot. They might be planning to sell your car to another dealer or to a wholesaler to auction. Auction prices are considerably lower than the retail price the dealership might get for selling your trade-in themselves. They will offer you a still lower price in order to make a profit selling your trade-in at auction.

Fight hard for a good realistic price. Indicate that it is the most important thing in the world to you, that you demand a good price for your used car. Do not begin to discuss the new car price until you have received a good price for your car. Be prepared to walk away in order to emphasize the importance of this issue. You must make the salesperson believe that you are a real buyer and that once the trade-in price is settled to your satisfaction, the rest of the transaction will go more smoothly. If the dealership agrees to a good price and then tries to take it back later, get mad and be prepared to walk out. If they give you a firm fixed price for your used car, they should stick with it. Dramatize the importance and the permanence of the price offered for your trade-in by writing it down with your big black felt marker. Have the salesperson initial that price or at least acknowledge it. Do not accept an allowance towards the purchase of a more expensive car. Get a hard price.

It would be ideal if you could easily get Blue Book wholesale for your used car trade-in. At best you won't get more than wholesale for your car from a dealership unless it is an unusual circumstance. Realistically, you may not get wholesale for your car. A good price would be Blue Book wholesale minus $300. Even more realistically you may be forced to settle for less than that. Again, remember that some cars are in demand and will bring more than "wholesale." Others are not well regarded and will get considerably less.

The best price for your used car might be obtained by selling it yourself. Usually cars sold through the paper or auto trader magazines advertise between Blue Book wholesale and Blue Book retail. A hot car in cherry shape may sell for more, while an car of average shape and popularity may sell for closer to wholesale or even below.

Remember, car sales staff immediately categorize buyers. They recognize people who fight hard for a good trade-in price, people who must have a good new car price, impulse buyers, etc. Your first job is to convince them that you are a person who needs a good price on the trade-in. They will assume that the remainder of the sale will be easy.

The New Car Price

You have done your homework and you know what your new car cost the dealer. A great price to aim for would be $300 above dealer's cost as calculated in Chapter 7. Remember, do not begin talking about new car price until you have a firm price for your trade-in — *not* an allowance, a firm price.

If the dealership demands that you discuss new cars first, or if they want to run a credit report, play at it for a while and then steer them back to the discussion of used car price. To emphasize this, toss them the keys to your trade-in and ask them repeatedly if they have looked at it and what the word is on the value of the car. Act as though you can't concentrate on anything else but the trade-in. Eventually they will give in just to keep the negotiating going and not let it bog down. Dealers rarely consider the used car price as a set price. They count on being able either to go back to this price later or to so confuse you that it will be forgotten.

Negotiate now for the best car price, using all the techniques you will soon read about. Fight here for your best price. Do not allow the dealer to cut the price given for your trade-in as you strive for a good price on the new car. Stop negotiating immediately, point to the figure on your pad (which the salesperson has already acknowledged) and insist that that number does not change. Once they acknowledge the figure again, resume the new car price negotiation. If you are forced to do this more than once, they will soon get the point and will no longer try to change the price given for your used car. Do not discuss financing or terms of payment or buy vs. lease here; go strictly after car price. Two things you should say over and over again are: "I really want to buy a car today," and "It is most important that I get a good price for this new car, if we do that, everything else will happen more easily."

At the end of the negotiations you should have a *fixed firm price* written down for the car — not a monthly payment, not an allowance deal with a used car, not a difference, but a *dollar value* for the new car including all the accessories you want. As with the trade-in, write the agreed upon price in your notebook with a black marker and get the salesperson to initial it if you can.

Remember, you may be forced to take some things you don't want to get items that you do want. Many items come only in packages. For instances, you may have to take tilt steering and cruise control when you buy the air-conditioning you want.

If you can couple a wholesale trade-in minus $300 with a wholesale plus $300 buy, you are an incredible car buyer and my hero.

Buying Special Packages/Options/Extras

This occurs in the office of the finance person. Remember, take only those extra items that you decided beforehand you needed. Think carefully about getting insurance, special exterior packages, rust prevention packages, etc. The best advice I can offer is to steer clear of the items offered in financing. These items are usually very highly priced with large markups. In the event you want something like an extended warranty, negotiate very strongly for it. Try to knock down the price by as much as two-thirds — this is not an unreasonable expectation given the mark-up. Threaten to terminate the whole deal unless you get it.

Financing

As we discussed earlier, it is important to feel confident about your financing. Get your financing through outside sources before you come into the showroom. This may be the financing you eventually choose. Alternatively, you may decide for one reason or another to take the dealer's financing. Show the lowest outside financing to the dealer and see if he can do better for you. Get him to quote his interest as an APR (annual percentage rate) and try not to get a "Rule of 78" interest payment (this will be explained in detail in the chapter on financing). This may be impossible, but if you keep the car until the end of the financing it won't make a difference. However there is an advantage to getting straight declining balance interest. If you do take a dealer's financing, make sure that you get a reasonable drop in interest to compensate for the disadvantages of "Rule of 78."

Remember, for best results, things should be done in a certain order. If you negotiate for your new car price before you have settled on your trade-in price, you face the probability of giving away your trade-in because you have fixed your allegiance on your new car.

It is important, actually critical, to do these four operations in the correct order. Do not mix them up or go from new car to financing to trade-in price to get a better car price if you take an extended warranty. After you have finished the test drive, have picked out a car you want, and are ready to go into the negotiating room and buy that vehicle, do it in the following order.

1. Settle the trade-in price. Don't do anything else; negotiate for the trade-in price.
2. After the trade-in price is settled, determine the new car equipment and purchase price.
3. In the finance room, determine what extras you want.
4. Determine how you are going to pay for the vehicle with the finance person. Determine payments, if any, and financing terms before you leave.

7

Calculating Dealer Costs

This next important operation, calculating dealer costs, can be done after a preliminary walk-through. It should be done before your serious visit when you come armed with all your research data, before you take your test drive, and before serious negotiations begin.

Wouldn't it be nice if you could know beforehand the dealer's cost for the new vehicle you just fell in love with? Wouldn't it be even nicer if you knew how much to offer him over his costs, a price he would just barely be able to accept?

Well, are you in luck. You can find out *exactly* what the car cost the dealership. This chapter provides guidelines to show what a dealership will reluctantly accept as a profit margin for their vehicle. Later chapters will tell you how to factor in such things as factory-to-customer rebates, hidden factory-to-dealer cash backs, and hold backs. With this information you will know exactly how hard you can push the salesperson to accept the price you offer.

NEW CAR COST FIGURES

First, let's work on a formula that will allow you to calculate what a vehicle cost the dealership. There are three ways to get this new car cost figure: (1) write to a service, (2) do the research yourself, or (3) calculate at the dealership using the factor.

1. You can write to a service that will quote you the dealer's cost for a vehicle with the options you request. Services like *Consumer Reports* charge ten or fifteen dollars per car for this information. The only problem with obtaining information this way is that if you are pricing three or four different cars, with different engines or options, you could spend a lot of money to be spoon fed the figures you want. It would be much cheaper to get the information yourself.

2. Look up the information yourself in appropriate publications such the annual April auto issue of *Consumer Reports* or Edmund's specialty auto books. Remember that you are paying yourself $150 per hour to do a good job on buying a car. That good job requires spending as little money as possible to get all the information you could ever need to make a good buy. This means doing your homework. Do this like a professional and have the peace of mind knowing that you have the accurate facts because you obtained them yourself.

    This research will give you both the dealer's cost and MSRP (manufacturer's suggested retail price) for the base car and the various options. All you have to do is to add the desired options to the dealer's cost for the base car. If this number differs from the sticker price on the vehicle, it may be that there has been a recent price increase by the manufacturer for the car.

    The MSRP is also called the sticker or list price. It is the undiscounted advertised price for the vehicle as recommended by the manufacturer.

3. Take the factor for the lease car and the factor for the options and use them in conjunction with the figures on the sticker. The factor is explained in detail below.

THE FACTOR

Another item you should get from the literature is the factor for the base car and for the options. This is a very useful piece of information and will allow you to calculate dealer's cost from the sticker price on the window of the new car. If the factor for the car you want is not given in your reference books, you can calculate it yourself by dividing the dealer's cost (as expressed in the above publications) by the published MSRP.

For example, let's say that the sticker price for the car is $12,000 and the dealer's cost is $10,000. The factor is .83 (10,000/12,000). This is very realistic, the factor is typically between .8 and .9. For instance, the factor for a Chevrolet Lumina is .86 for the car and .85 for the options. A factor of .85 means that the car cost the dealer 85% of the sticker price on the car. In other words, a factor of .85 means a 15% profit on the car because the dealer paid 85% of the sticker price for the car. If you want to get 25% off the sticker price, you will find that the dealer will not treat you seriously because that is 10% below his cost.

Car prices may change, but the factors usually stay the same for a given vehicle from year to year. The factor is very helpful to know as you negotiate. It will give you a great feeling of confidence to be able to critically evaluate any salesperson's statement that she can't give you your proposed price because it is below her costs. You will immediately know if there is any truth to that statement.

UNDERSTANDING STICKER PRICE

Here is how to interpret and utilize the information on the car's main sticker, which is usually placed on the side of every new car that is up for sale. In many cases there is more than one sticker, a main one and one or more smaller stickers. These smaller stickers deal with extras such as a wax job, special wire wheels, or pinstriping.

Since you have come to the showroom with your homework done and you know the factor for your car and its options, you can calculate dealer's cost from the sticker as follows:

1. Locate the main price sticker on the car.
2. Disregard the other small stickers charging for special services.
3. Locate the base price for the car (without any extras) and enter the figure in (A) below. This number is usually located on the top of the sticker.
4. Total up all the extras you know you want and enter this figure in (B) below.
5. Write down the factor for your base car in (C) below.
6. Write down the factor for your extras in (D) below.
7. Completely disregard any charge for AMU or ADMU, which are simple additional dealer markups (extra profit).
8. Disregard all charges for things you don't want, such as a wax job, undercoating, etc.

(A) $_____
(B) $_____
(C) $_____
(D) $_____

The dealer's cost for this car with its extras but without the special services like wax and pin stripes is

$(A \times C) + (B \times D)$ + transportation (from the sticker).

Here is an example. You want to buy a Mitsubishi Eclipse, the GS 16v model. The published factor for the car is .87 and the published factor for the extras (air conditioning, etc.) is .82.

THE LIST PRICE FOR THE BASE CAR IS	$13,439
AIR CONDITIONING LISTS FOR	$ 811
POWER STEERING AND DEFROST LIST FOR	$ 119
ALLOY WHEELS LIST FOR	$ 319

You would calculate the dealer's cost for the car with AC, power windows, rear window defroster, and alloy wheels as:

(car factor x MSRP for car) + (options factor x MSRP for options) =

(.87 x $13,439) + (.82 x ($811 + $119 + $315) =

(.87 x $13,439) + (.82 x $1,245) =

$11,692 + $1,021 =

$12,713

Also add destination charges (transportation) to the final calculation. This figure is on the main sticker on the car. On this car they are $343.

$12,713 + $343 = $13,056.

Always add destination charges at the end of your calculation. The factor does not affect these transportation charges.

Compare this to the total sticker price for the car plus the options plus the transportation:

$13,439 + ($811 + $119 + $315) + $343 =

$13,439 + $1,245 + $343 =

$15,027

If the dealership sold the car at list price, its gross profit on this segment of the transaction would be list price less his cost.

$15,027 - $13,056 = $1,971

Granted, the dealership has other costs, but do you really want all of this profit to come out of your pocket?

CONSTRUCTING A BID

In negotiating for the above Mitsubishi, the price to aim for the would be the dealer's cost plus $300 profit for the dealership. That would be $13,056 plus $300 profit for the dealership or $13,356. In order to end up here, initially bid $13,256 ($100 less) as a place to start. Now, if the Eclipse is a hot car or if it is a seller's market, you may well have to pay more than this bare bones price. But at least you know where to start. Offering a few hundred dollars over a dealer's base costs puts the salesperson in a terrible fix. Your opening price is not so ridiculous that he can just ignore it. It is just low enough to lower his expectations and still keep him interested.

Some dealerships will try to itemize out their costs for such things as advertising and charge you for them separately on top of the agreed-upon price. These costs are certainly a part of the dealership's operating expenses, but whether you should pay them as a separate item on the car is another matter. In addition, the dealership has other costs that are to come out of that $300 in profit you are trying to leave them, like the commissions and the floor plan (financing) that they pay on the car. But that's not your problem; that's their problem.

To summarize: you can find out exactly what the car cost the dealership. You can also determine the factor that will allow you to calculate their exact cost using the sticker on the car. This is useful in case there has been a price increase since the list you read was published. Knowing this information is like playing poker and being able to see some of your opponent's cards; it gives you a great advantage.

From your calculations, you can begin to negotiate in order to determine how much money over cost the dealership will accept for the new car. Fight to limit them to only $300 over their cost. As you can see from our sample figures earlier, this is a substantial savings for you.

With all of your homework done, financing arranged, an evaluation of your trade-in completed, and a decision made on what to offer the dealer for your dream car, this is the time to visit the dealership for a test drive of your chosen chariot.

8

The Test Drive

There is nothing more pleasant for a car buyer than the test drive. It is usually a time of minimum pressure and maximum enjoyment, but for you, the serious buyer, the test drive should also be the beginning of an extensive evaluation which will show you if the car you have chosen is one you will be happy with.

People who are unhappy with the car they have so carefully chosen can often trace their problems right back to something they didn't notice or failed to seriously consider during the test drive. As with anything having to do with cars, the stories abound: One friend never uses his BMW's fifth gear because he can't reliably shift into it from fourth. An acquaintance is afraid to drive on freeways because her new car won't accelerate fast enough; another has a terrible time getting out of her car's seats because the lateral side supports on the driver's side impede her graceful exit ... and the list goes on.

Take the test drive very seriously. Enjoy it, but don't get so caught up in the excitement of buying a new car that you are careless. Allow yourself plenty of time; perhaps an hour for a complete inspection, preferably of the exact car, with all the options, that you want to take home. Of course a salesperson will be there with his own agenda and goals, but don't let this deter you from your appointed task. When he sees your detailed checklist he will know that you are a buyer to be reckoned with.

The test drive usually occurs soon after you arrive at the dealership. Most buyers can't wait. Before you get behind the wheel of a car that looks just like the one you want, make sure it is exactly the one you want, complete, if possible, with every option you want. Also, before the test drive, you should ask the salesperson to have your trade-in evaluated while you're gone. It is best not to be present when they find all the items with which they will devalue your old car and justify their low offer. If you are not there you are in a psychologically stronger position later to negotiate for a better price.

The salesperson who invariably accompanies you during your test drive may now seem more like a guide, more chatty and relaxed. But, for strategic reasons, consider the test drive as another part of your negotiations. Tell him only what he needs to know. Don't be too negative about the car unless you have already decided that you absolutely don't want it. Also, avoid giving buying signals. It is best to remain coolly analytical and to appear neutral at this time. There is nothing wrong, however, with showing him that you are knowledgeable and have really done your homework.

Don't forget that your evaluation of the car really began with your own research so that now you are competent to say something more than, "It's really a beauty." You are in a position to assess, first hand, the validity and relevance of the professional ratings. For instance: does its reported lack of power at high speeds pose a problem for you? Perhaps not if you are a slow city driver. It will take time to think, consider, and evaluate your priorities. Above all, be willing and determined to take your time. With these factors in mind, you are ready to start your test drive.

THE PRE-DRIVE INSPECTION

◆ Do you love the exterior? If not, you should look at another vehicle.
◆ Do you love its interior ambiance, or is it just adequate?
◆ Are the doors so heavy or the door handles so awkward it is a strain to use them?
◆ Do the doorstops keep the door open easily? (Of special concern on larger cars.)
◆ Can you lock and unlock the doors easily from the inside?
◆ Are you comfortable in the car? Do your feet fit the pedals?
◆ Test the seats in all positions. Can you get in and out of them easily? Are they adequately adjustable?
◆ Do the seats have good back support?
◆ Is the headrest adequately adjustable?
◆ Does your head hit the roof? (This may prevent you from buying a car with a sun roof. Sun roofs are a little lower than normal roofs.)
◆ Are the lights, wiper switches, cruise control, radio, etc. easy to find and use?
◆ Is the horn easily found and easy to use?
◆ Is the interior lighting adequate?
◆ Are there map lights? Do they work well?
◆ Will the lights automatically turn off when the engine shuts down? (This prevents draining of the battery if the lights are left on.)

◆ Can you easily read the gauges, radio, and computer readouts, both day and night?
◆ Are the controls usable or are they too complicated?
◆ Are both mirrors adjustable from the driver's side?
◆ Are there adequate pockets? For instance, where would you put a map, a book of maps, a pocketbook, your garage opener, extra keys, cigarettes, and other small items?
◆ Are there vanity mirrors on both visors of the car? Are they lit?
◆ Are there coin slots and cup holders?
◆ Is there a front seat console for tapes, CDs, etc.?
◆ Can you easily attach and adjust the seat belts?
◆ Can you easily see over the hood?
◆ Can you see over the back and front of the car?
◆ Can you easily see into the back seat to talk to others or watch your kids?
◆ Are there air bags on both sides?

THE MOVING INSPECTION

◆ Did the car start easily? Turn the car on and off several times.
◆ Is the steering column easy to lock and unlock?
◆ Does the radio work well? Is the sound adequate for you?
◆ Does the car maneuver easily at low speeds getting out of the parking lot?
◆ How is the turning radius? Can you make a U-turn in the road?
◆ Can you parallel park easily?
◆ How is the acceleration? Can you zip around in comfort and in control of the situation?
◆ Is there enough acceleration to easily fit into traffic — even freeway traffic? How about going up a hill?
◆ Is the car powerful enough? Does it pass easily? Does it have enough power to get up hills when loaded?
◆ Is there power at both low speeds and higher speeds? Many cars have drive trains that are fine at lower speeds and die at higher speeds.
◆ Is the car so big it feels like a boat, or so small it feels vulnerable?
◆ If the transmission is manual, is it smooth? How does it feel while shifting? Is it too easy to mix up the gears?
◆ If the transmission is automatic, does it shift smoothly and at the right times?
◆ Is the steering responsive at higher speeds? Does it understeer or oversteer around corners?

♦ Do the brakes work smoothly without needing a lot of pressure? Would you feel comfortable in a panic stop?
♦ Is the car quiet when stopped, moving, and accelerating? Turn off the radio to really hear it.
♦ How is the wind noise at higher speeds?
♦ Is the car stable at cruising speeds?
♦ Is the ride too hard or too soft? Do you need a different suspension?
♦ Does it "porpoise" when hitting bumps?
♦ How is the vibration at high speeds and on rougher roads?
♦ Does the engine idle smoothly at stops?
♦ Can it tow anything that you have to tow?
♦ Is this the exact car you are buying or a similar one with significant differences (like a different engine, etc.)?
♦ Is visibility good in all directions? Do you notice any major blind spots?
♦ Are the instruments visible? Can you easily reach all the features, including the radio, windshield wipers, lights, temperature controls, dash, etc.?

THE POST-DRIVE INSPECTION

After you have driven the car and are back at the dealership look at the following:
♦ Will the vehicle fit in your garage?
♦ Is the trunk adequate?
♦ Try the back seat. Is it comfortable for both sitting and reclining?
♦ Do both front seats recline?
♦ Can you open the hood easily?
♦ Is the motor easily set up for servicing? (This is of particular interest to those of us who change oil, etc.)
♦ Are the oil, water, power steering fluid, etc., marked and easily accessible?

At the end of the test drive, you should know if you must have this car at any price, if you want it only at the right price, or if you still want it at all. If your answer was you only want it at the right price, which is the only satisfying and "no regrets" way to buy a car, you are now ready to have some fun negotiating for it.

9

Getting the Best Price for Your Trade-In

Okay, this is it. It's time to decide whether or not to buy the car. You have done your homework, seen their products, read all the literature available, seen what you can afford (and what the experts say about your choice of vehicles), and finally taken a test drive. Now is the time to decide: are you going to buy this car or not?

If the answer is "No" or "I don't know yet," don't feel pressured by or beholden to the dealership or salesperson. Get your keys back and walk off the lot as quickly as possible and go somewhere either to see other vehicles or to decide what to do. But whatever you do, don't do your thinking in the dealership's negotiating offices.

NEGOTIATIONS

If the answer is "Yes," now is the time to remember to stick to your order of operations and concentrate on getting the best price for your trade-in. Why? Because most car buyers use their trade-in money as the down payment for their new car. Getting the best trade-in price for your vehicle is critical to making a good car buy. The standard tactic of most dealerships is to give you a reasonable price on their new car and to absolutely destroy and lowball you on your trade-in. Don't be misled by low new car prices alone. Your first order of business is to get the very best price for your used car. You know what it is worth because you did all the homework and have a clear evaluation. Now let's go after getting that price from some pretty hard characters.

Here is the way to achieve this goal. First, examine and change your attitude. You must appear colder, more detached, and more irritable than you did during the test drive. Allow yourself to be lured into the salesperson's office to discuss a *possible* car purchase. Be a little reluctant, and go at his insistence. During the test drive you should have been a little more mild-mannered and a lot less knowledgeable than you will appear now. It is always best to appear naive at first to throw off the sales staff who make fast judgments about people and to gradually appear to be more knowledgeable and tougher as the negotiations progress.

Remember, the dealership's salespeople are trained to classify car buyers in various ways. One classification is the TRADE-IN BUYER. This type of person is concerned primarily with getting a good price for his trade-in. Once this is taken care of, he is less concerned about car payments, new car price, or any other issue. Thus dealerships give him a good price for his trade-in and make their money by dealing hard on the other parts of the auto transaction. Your goal at this point in the transaction is to convince your salesperson that you are a TRADE-IN BUYER. Later you will convince him that you are a NEW CAR PRICE BUYER. A NEW CAR PRICE BUYER is one who is interested primarily in the price of the new car and will not concentrate on trade-in price or any other issue. Your goal is to be a TRADE-IN BUYER when it suits you, then to switch and become a NEW CAR PRICE BUYER later in the transaction.

Once you have begun to change your attitude and are in the office, reiterate that you would like to buy a car *today* but that you want the best price for your trade-in before you discuss the new car. Tell your salesperson that if this point is handled to your satisfaction, everything else will go smoothly. You want him to mark you as a TRADE-IN BUYER and treat you as one. Remember, a TRADE-IN BUYER is given a great price on her trade-in in the hopes that she will be locked into buying a new car and will provide the profit the dealership needs in the other areas of the transaction. The salesperson hopes to make his profit on the new car purchase, the financing, and the financing extras. Let him think this will happen for now.

I can't stress this enough; get *their* price on your trade-in first. Don't give them a definite figure of what you want. It is a general principle of negotiation that whoever mentions price first loses. Indicate how important it is for you to get a great price. If you can, send the salesperson back to his boss many times by indicating that their price for your trade-in is unacceptable. If necessary, get huffy, upset, and appear to have your feelings hurt. Keep saying the trade-in price is critical to buying a new car. Don't give them your bottom line figure early. Reiterate that you really want to get a car today and ask them why they won't let you do so. Remember, you want to be classified as a TRADE-IN BUYER.

If anyone came with you to approve the car choice and pick the color of the upholstery, ask them to leave until you call them. (Obviously, you want to work this out in advance of your arrival at the showroom). This is the time to ask the person who is approving the choice but would not be good in a negotiation to go away and come back later after the car has been bought. This may be tough to do, because you surely don't want to hurt this person's feelings. Is it worthwhile paying hundreds of dollars not to hurt their feelings?

Make sure that you have all the details of your trade-in handy to support your claim that the car is a creampuff. You should have brought details on extra features, recent repair records, etc. Show these details even if the car is not a creampuff, but later settle for a lower price. Remember your strongest negotiating posture at this point is one of a trade-in buyer who loves the old car and is a little irrational about it.

If used car prices are high, remind the salesperson that you are aware of that fact. State that you know your car is a creampuff and you know used car prices are high, so they will be able to sell it immediately. Tell them you want their best figure *now*.

After they have given you their first price (which will most certainly be low and unsatisfactory), try a new technique. Simply say, "You have to do better than that if this conversation is to continue." Send the salesperson back for a better figure. Send him back frequently for a better price. Think of it as exercise; it's good for him and good for you. My rule of thumb is that a salesperson should make a total of five to ten trips back and forth between you and the boss for a standard car transaction. Emphasize that this trade-in price is critical and the only thing standing between you and a new car purchase.

If the price comes back low, ask to see his boss or the person who evaluated the vehicle. Tell your salesperson that if you are treated right you may come back for future vehicles as well. Stick to the topic of used car price; don't meaningfully discuss new car price at this time.

Hold fast to the price you want for your trade-in. Don't accept his low "auction" price. (Your research will tell you what auction price really is, or at least what wholesale price is based on car condition, mileage, etc.)

Remember, you came in late — one to two hours before closing. You will be there for several hours after closing. They are tired, you are not. Let the negotiations go slowly. You want *them* to be the ones to try to speed things up by giving concessions. The longer this deal takes and the later it goes, the better it is for you. Fatigue on their part will make for better prices for you. Tire them out, make them want to get the transaction over with. Make absolutely sure that they consider you a real buyer; keep saying, "I really want to buy a car today."

Chapter 12 lists a series of techniques or tactics designed to help you get your best deal. For this part of your car-buying process, skip ahead and read about the techniques, BROKEN RECORD and YOU HAVE TO DO BETTER THAN THAT. They will be of great use to you here.

In a perverse way, salespeople expect you to be unreasonable when defending your trade-in. Don't disappoint them. Hold fast initially, don't give your expected price first but try for Blue Book wholesale for your car and then let your price slip below wholesale. If your car is a wreck, you will get a much lower price. If it is cherry with low mileage you can get closer to wholesale. Remember, a great price is about $300 less than Blue Book wholesale. If your car is a hot vehicle you may get it, but be prepared to accept less.

FIRM PRICE VS. ALLOWANCES

Get a fixed firm price for your trade-in; don't settle for an allowance. An allowance is where the dealer says "I will give you $2000 for your car *if* you buy this particular upscale model *at full price.* You eventually don't know what you got for your car or what you paid for the new car. It all becomes very confusing. Compartmentalize each individual transaction; a trade-in negotiation is a trade-in negotiation and should not be tied in with any other part of the transaction. If you are offered an allowance, get a little huffy, and get back to price. Make it clear that you will not accept an allowance but will proceed with the transaction only after a firm price for your trade-in has been agreed on.

This is a final reminder. Be persistent; be firm; threaten to walk out. Don't just melt away at the first touch of dealer resistance. If they won't give in at all, walk out and try your tactics at a different dealership. But always indicate that you are a real buyer and that you "want to buy a car *today.*"

Remember, you have the edge—you are the customer and it is your money.

10

Who Has the Advantage?

As you have thought about trying to get a good price for your trade-in, you might have wondered if there is anyway for you to come out on top.

It's always nice to know who has the advantage in any situation. Football teams think theirs is a home field advantage. Poker players feel a sense of comfort with their backs facing the wall. So, you may wonder who in the car-buying arena has the best odds. My feeling is that the edge lies strongly with an informed buyer. Let's look at the advantages that both sellers and buyers have and then decide how to use the system to give you, the buyer, the edge.

THE CAR DEALER'S ADVANTAGES

Here are the advantages that auto sellers have:
1. The salesperson knows and is the expert in the field. He knows the product line. He knows the economy for selling. He knows options, prices, and the million and one relevant details.
2. The salesperson sells every day. He understands people because he practices on customers every day. He knows what it takes to bring together a reluctant buyer and the car of her dreams. He is very practiced at making a car transaction happen.

   You, on the other hand, are there on a one-shot buy faced with the major decision of spending a major part of your disposable income. You probably haven't prepared and may just be starting your car-buying process. He can spot all these items and discover what it is that will make you commit to a new car. He is naturally attuned to discovering these things, and his further sales training on how to sell you a car more efficiently will work in his favor.

3. He has the personality for high-pressure sales. Good salespeople are not shrinking violets. Car salespeople are smooth, aggressive people who can force or defuse a confrontation. In many cases, they can impose their will on a customer and control him or her. They are drawn to sales in part by the strength of their personalities. As a rule, they have much stronger personalities than the general population.

4. You are out of your element and on his turf. It is common knowledge that dogs are tougher and meaner on their home turf and are more hesitant and passive on someone else's property. People have similar tendencies. This means that you, the customer, will tend to defer to the salesman's pushy personality more in his salesroom than you would in your living room. I can't imagine that you would allow yourself to be yelled at and intimidated on your own porch as you will allow yourself to be in a car showroom.

5. You probably need a car right now. This means that you have an immediate need that only the car dealer can meet. If you wait until the last minute, when your car is breaking down, to go out and buy a new car, you will lose a lot of your bargaining power. It is tough to fight hard for a good price for your trade-in when it isn't running. It is hard to threaten to walk out of a showroom if your car won't start.

6. The dealer is focused and decisive. Even if he really needs a car, the average person is torn by a lot of questions: Should I buy a new car? Can I really afford it? Should I fix up my old clunker and make do? The salesperson is single-minded. He wants to sell this person a car *today* at the *maximum* profit. He is not wishy-washy. He has his goals laid out for him and knows what he has to do to achieve these goals.

7. He has reserve troops. If he can't sell you a car because of a personality clash or another problem, there are other salespeople who can and will. If he needs other help, he has closers and general managers to convince you, to wear you out, or to supply other information. He also has literature, displays, and, of course, the car with which you are in love.

8. They created the system. The salesperson knows the system and how it works. As a consequence of setting up the present car-buying system, the car selling industry has designed it to work efficiently to separate you from the maximum amount of your money. This system must be very efficient, because all the car companies use essentially the same system.

9. His authority is limited; yours is binding. This is a great tactic used extensively by many great negotiating powers. No matter what you, the customer, say, you are held to your word. Yet no matter what the salesperson says, he is not held to anything because he has to check with his boss. If you change your mind or back away, you are openly challenged and called a wimp or a dishonest individual. If he backs away from a promise, it is because his big bad mean boss won't let him earn an honest living for his wife and seventeen children.

THE CAR BUYER'S ADVANTAGES

I know it sounds as if all of the advantages belong to the dealer, but there are some great advantages that belong to car buyers. These advantages are so strong that car sellers had to devise a whole system to come out ahead. BUT you have to be informed to be able to use these natural advantages.

You Pick the Time and Place

You can pick the time and place to buy a car. While the car seller is stuck waiting in his showroom, you can go to any dealer you want, anytime you want. This means that you can buy a car when it is convenient for you, when you are well rested, and when the time is right for buying. These are very important factors in an auto negotiation.

Obviously, only you can determine these first two items. But I can tell you definitively the best time for buying a car. The best time for buying a car is one to two hours prior to the dealership's closing time. The best days are those near the end of the month, during bad economic times, or during a rainy weekend. If you can combine all of these, your timing is perfect. This is the key time to buy, since it gives you a few hours to test drive the car you want, inspect the car, and have your trade-in appraised before you get down to serious negotiations. Salespeople, like other people, like to get home early. In the middle of the day, they will sit and wait and negotiate until you give in. The later you keep the sales staff after hours, the more they want to finish the sale quickly.

Buying a car at the end of the month or the end of the quarter adds even more of an advantage. All dealers are rated by their monthly volume. At the end of the month they are more willing to give way on price to get one more sale.

Slow economic times, Christmas week, and other national holidays are also times when car sellers are more anxious to make a deal and will bend more under pressure.

Therefore, your advantage in buying a car is to buy it when the sellers are tired, distracted, or in need of a sale. They can't pick a time to sell a car, but you can pick a time to buy a car. This is a big edge — don't underestimate it.

You Can Walk Out

You can walk out at any time — the seller can't. As long as you stay there and argue and negotiate, the salesperson must also stay. He can't walk out and leave you alone in the middle of the showroom, but you can get mad at any point and walk out and he is powerless to stop you. You can always walk out in the middle of a negotiation and force the salesperson to run out to the parking lot to try and coax you to continue the dialogue. Saying that you will leave if the salesperson doesn't get serious is a threat that he can't match. The ultimate test of how far you can go is to see if the sales force actually tries to prevent you from going. You can leave a negotiation and come back the next day, and open the dialogue again; they can't. If the salesperson is being confrontational or pushy, your implied threat of leaving is often enough to control his outrageous behavior and to force him to make his best bid quickly — before you disappear.

You have the power to initiate selling and to terminate it, the salesperson can't do either. This is another big edge.

It's Your Money

You are the customer ... *it is your money*. Sales staff are trained to respect the customer as king. They don't like it, but they do realize that the customer has the money and that they have to defer to her in some ways in order to get it. The salesperson is limited to acting in a certain way and to following a "script," but you can talk or act pretty well the way you want, and he has to put up with it. You can make ridiculous statements, change your mind, and get away with it because you are the customer and it's your money. You can directly remind the sales staff of this point. Say, "I am the customer and it is my money." You have a right to spend your money *as* you wish, *when* you wish. You are in charge of the money, and they have to defer to you if they have any hope of getting it.

Your Power Grows with Time Spent

As the negotiations progress, the dealer's position gets weaker and your position gets stronger. I know that most people feel that as the negotiations progress and proceed towards completion, their position weakens. That is just not true. In the early stages of a negotiation, if you walk out, the salesperson has not wasted much time on you and won't regret your leaving very much. But as she puts in time and effort and the negotiations progress, she will become more concerned about losing a probable sale. At that point, she may have even told her boss that "the sale is in the bag." Her job or ranking in the company may hinge on just a few more sales so she just doesn't want to fail after she has invested so much time.

The finance person is in an even more difficult position. After a car has been sold, if the sale falls through in finance he has to answer not only to the general manager, but to the salesperson as well—who was already banking on the sale.

A car buyer's power increases right up to the point where he puts his signature on the contract, then it immediately decreases. This means that the longer you keep a salesperson tied up negotiating and dealing with you, the better deal you can drive (since he has invested more time in the selling of this vehicle). So take your time, don't rush, keep him overtime, deal towards the end of the month, pick weak economic times and rainy weekends, and believe that as the negotiations progress and he gets more interested, your power increases.

TIME IN NEGOTIATION VS. POWER

Customer's Power

Increasing Time in Negotiation

The above chart graphically shows this. Your position is weakest when you first walk in and the salesperson has not yet qualified you as a real honest-to-goodness customer. As you talk and convince him that you are a real prospect your value to him increases. Therefore, your power to demand and command increases. After all, he doesn't want to lose a potential sale. As you agree on items like trade-in price, new car price, etc., you become a very probable sale and, therefore, even more valuable. By this time the sales staff will probably be treating you with kid gloves.

Deadlock is an important negotiating situation in which the salesperson and you can't reach an agreement. You can deliberately create a deadlock and resolve it later if you wish. You can give it up for a concession of his later, or you can allow the deadlock not to be broken and just walk out. Don't fear a lack of an agreement on all points. It is not a sign of weakness or lack of skill. It is actually the opposite. Deadlocks are especially useful if he has classified you as a real buying prospect. In that case he will bend over backwards to reach an agreement and break the deadlock.

You become the strongest just as you have agreed on everything and are about to sign. Your negotiating position immediately plummets once you sign. For example, did you ever try to demand anything more after you had agreed to a contract and signed on the dotted line?

Never worry about losing control as the negotiation proceeds. In actuality you don't get weaker; you get stronger. The benefit of getting stronger is that you do not have to take abuse or give back benefits. Further into the negotiations you actually become stronger and can demand more or can make sure that what was promised to you is delivered.

To show this very clearly, consider what a salesperson will have to explain to his boss if he is kept two hours overtime to close a sale and the sale falls through at the last minute. Even worse, what will the finance and insurance (F & I) person say to the salesperson and manager if after everyone has been kept overtime for two hours the F & I person loses the sale?

In conclusion, even though the sales organization seems to have a huge edge, on closer inspection that is not true. You are the customer and it is your money. You can do what you want and buy where you will. My feelings are that a well-informed, capable car buyer has the edge, *absolutely*. But it is difficult to convince most buyers of that. Why? Because most car salespeople come across as formidable, intimidating opponents.

11

Dealer Tactics and How to Counter Them

How did he do it? How did that last salesman twist your mind into a pretzel and convince you to buy that car, which wasn't the one you came in for? That car you bought only five years ago; that car you didn't need; that car you are trading in right now to avoid further hassles. He did it so skillfully, you weren't even aware of what was happening. Well, it is no great mystery. As I said in the previous chapter, professional salespeople have the edge on their own turf with an *uninformed* consumer. They learn tricks and techniques from the masters, spend years trying to apply them, and even longer discovering the type of person who is most susceptible to each technique.

Knowledge is power. If you know when a "technique" is being used on you, then it becomes easier to ignore it and singlemindedly get on with your business—buying the car of your choice at the lowest possible price. You cannot be confused or bamboozled if you can dismiss anything which even remotely resembles a manipulative technique. Once you recognize them, you might even want to learn to use them yourself. Some might come in handy if you try to sell your own car.

The following is a list of some of the most common and most successful techniques used by professional salespeople.

TAKE IT OR LEAVE IT

Take it or leave it is the standard marketing policy all Americans have grown up with. You go to a restaurant or a furniture or clothing store and you "take it or leave it" at the price marked on the item. However, in the auto business, you don't have to take it or leave it. You can negotiate for it. You can, of course, leave it and later come back and take it. It is a good negotiating practice always to leave it before you take it. The tactic is usually a ploy to force you into an early decision, but eventually it may really be the way it is. You'll never know unless you test it.

MAKING YOU FEEL GUILTY

"I really need the sales," or "You're just wasting my time," or "Are you serious about buying this car?" or "I may lose my job if I don't make this sale," or "I consider you a friend," or " One more sale this week will win me a trip to Hawaii," pleads the salesperson.

If you find that any one of the above plays on your emotions makes you feel guilty, you will be had. Remember, the problems of the dealership staff are their problems, not yours. Remember why you are there; you want to buy a car. You are not there to make a friend or solve the world's social problems. Showing empathy will merely encourage further appeals. Hard as it may be, try to keep a businesslike distance between you and the salesperson.

WRITE MAKES RIGHT

Somehow or other if things are written down, we are not as apt to question them. The written word has a certain power of legitimacy. Car dealers are armed with an array of written facts, figures, forms, and rules which they say are etched in stone. You should always assume that anything written is negotiable, that prices are meant to be tested, and that any item can be adjusted. If you do your homework, you will know what all items cost, which costs are fixed and which are not. The fact that a dealer has something written down doesn't mean it is true. Question everything.

THE CALIFORNIA APPROACH

"What do I have to do to get you to buy a car today?" the salesperson queries, over and over again — each time more forcefully, until the buyer's objections are understood and countered one by one. Hopefully, the buyer will peacefully sign on the dotted line just to end the pressure.

The counter to this is to *know* what a good deal is, ask for it, and demand that the salesperson stop pressuring you. The broken record technique (explained later) works well as a deterrent to the California approach.

GOOD GUY/BAD GUY

In this scenario, the salesperson becomes your friend and helps escort you through a maze of roadblocks. His sales manager keeps bringing up problems and your friendly salesperson helps you to solve them — usually by having you give way on point after point. Your best tactic is to keep a formal distance between you and the salesperson and to indicate that good guy/bad guy is such an old tactic that you are surprised that anybody is still using it.

CONTROL THROUGH QUESTIONING

Since the person who asks the questions and demands answers is in control of the situation, it might as well be you. The salesperson does have a need to ask some qualifying questions to find out what it is you need, want, and can afford, but he has no right to demand answers or to answer each of your questions with a closing question. For instance:

YOU: Can you get me that car in red?

SALESPERSON: If I do, will you buy the car today?

NOTE: His response shows that he is asking you to make a decision about buying prematurely. Your reply should be:

YOU: I would like an answer to my question please: can you get me that car in red? When I get my answer, I will be better able to determine if I am going to buy or not.

THE TEAM APPROACH

In some dealerships, there are layers of salespeople. Each layer has a different responsibility. One greets you, another takes you for the test drive, another starts the sale, and yet another closes it. Sometimes several salespeople will gang up on you in sequence and work on you until you wear out. The best way to handle this is not to allow more than one salesperson at a time to work with you, and to arrive so late that there are few salespeople around. Don't allow them to doubleteam you. Leave if you can't control this situation.

DELAY

Sales staff can extend negotiations in several ways: by running in lots of other salespeople, losing your keys, or having you wait around so long that you get anxious or tired and just want to consummate the deal as quickly as possible. However, they will only do this if you have signaled that you are susceptible to this type of treatment. So when you are sitting and waiting for the salesperson to come back with a counter offer, make them uneasy. Get up, walk around, go outside. The customer who can successfully control the pace of negotiations is more likely to have them go his way. A typical delaying scenario can go something like this:

SALESPERSON: Your credit report seems to be presenting some problems. It will take us about sixty minutes for us to check with our bank. Why don't you have a cup of coffee in the reception area and we'll get back to you soon?

YOU: My credit is fine, and I'm late for dinner. Why don't I just go home and have you call me tomorrow when you finish your investigation.

SALESPERSON (panicking — he is afraid you will walk off): Wait just a minute; let's see if I can speed this up.

GOING GOING GONE

Saying that they only have one car left like the one you want is a great way to force you to make an immediate, perhaps premature, decision. By making you feel that your choice is their hottest car and that the supply is limited, a salesperson thinks he can force you into a commitment. If this tactic it tried, you should be willing to let your dream car go if everything else isn't exactly right.

Another version of going going gone is the line, "This deal is good for one day only … TODAY!" The only response to this variation is to say, "Well then, I may miss it." A deal is good for as long as anybody wants it to be good. There is usually no reason for a time limit on any offer. Call their bluff by adhering to your own agenda. If you lose it, you lose it.

"ONLY THE PAYMENTS ARE IMPORTANT … RIGHT?"

WRONG! Sometimes, the real cost of a car can be obscured when the salesperson says, "We both know that the only important thing is to get your monthly payments down as low as possible." Beware of this ploy. Before you know it, you will have a lower payment, a much longer payment time, and a higher down payment. If you are not careful, you won't even know the price you actually paid for the new car. This tactic is usually used when the buyer stalls on a high price because of sticker shock. Never worry about payments until you talk to the finance person. Always know what you actually paid for the car, and always fight hard for the lowest car price.

"ONLY THE DIFFERENCE IN PRICE IS IMPORTANT … RIGHT?"

Wrong again. Often the salesperson will try to convince you all that really matters is the difference between the new car price and the trade-in price. Your salesperson is deliberately trying to confuse you. In actuality the difference between the new car and trade-in price *is* important. But it is even more important to know the *exact price* of each to avoid being confused. If you are not careful, every time you get the new car price to drop, somehow or other the agreed upon price for the used car will suddenly drop also. Determine the price of each separately and keep track of each separately. This will prevent you from becoming confused as the buying progresses. It will also prevent you from losing money on your trade-in.

It is also easy to be confused by allowances: "I will allow you $____ towards the purchase of your new car at $____." Get fixed, firm prices for each item in the negotiation. The price of your new car should not be dependent on the allowance for your trade-in. Allowances never work for you.

LOWBALLING

To enhance their profits, car dealers usually strongly lowball trade-ins. This is because their profits on the new car are sometimes limited by the amount of money banks will lend towards new car transactions. Remember, there are several parts to a transaction, and even though you get a low price for the new car, you still must get a reasonable price for your used car. Lowballing is used when the salesperson determines that you are very concerned about new car price but are relatively unconcerned about what you get for your trade-in. He will try to focus your attention on a reasonable price for the new car, and yet lowball you on the price of your trade-in. While your attention is focused on saving hundreds of dollars on the new car, you may forget to watch the trade-in sale and can easily lose thousands.

The reverse could also be true. If the salesperson feels you are adamant about getting a good price for your trade-in (for the down payment on a new car), he will give you an unbelievable price for your trade-in, charge you above list for the new car, and tie both prices together as a package deal. To counter this, first make the salesperson believe the only thing of importance is a good price for your trade-in. *After* you get it, make him realize that the only important thing is a low new car price — but don't give back the great trade-in price. Having previously written down the agreed upon trade-in price will be very helpful, especially if you have had the salesperson acknowledge it at some point in the transaction.

BAIT AND SWITCH

If you are not careful, you can walk into a dealership to buy the car that you have thoroughly researched, the one that suits your needs and price structure, and come out instead with one that you just fell in love with. When you find yourself switched, for any reason (perhaps away from a very low-priced sale car), leave until you can think your way through the new situation and do the necessary homework.

VERBAL PROMISES

During your buy, a lot of things will be promised to you verbally. Every time something is offered, *write it down* and keep a list. Even better, have the salesperson or his boss initial the items agreed upon. Save this list for the closing when they will probably try to take back some of the items they have given you.

LIMITED AUTHORITY

Having a lack of authority would seem to make a person's negotiating position weaker, but, in actuality, the best negotiating position is to have no authority at all. Then you can back off any agreement you have made by merely indicating that you aren't authorized to make it. Automobile salespeople operate very effectively by relying on this lack of authority. This allows them to make an agreement with you and also say, "My boss may not go for this." You, however, are expected to be able to make and stick to all your agreements. Ask the salesperson at the onset of negotiations if he has the authority to make a deal. His usual response will be either not to answer, to answer or ask another question, or to be evasive. At this point, indicate that if he has no authority, you want to deal with someone who has. Do not let his lack of authority control you.

GETTING YOU TO SAY "YES ... YES ... YES."

The theory is that if you say yes to a long line of questions, it will then become easier for you to say yes to accepting a less than adequate deal. When this happens, get obstinate and say no or, "Maybe, if ..." a few times. Other options are to change the subject or to get him to say yes to one of your demands.

NIBBLES

Car dealers are very good at asking for small concession after small concession. Before you know it, you have given away the store. If this is happening, *counter nibble*. Don't give away anything without asking for something back. For instance, if the salesperson wants you to agree to a higher price before he presents the offer to his boss, use it as an opportunity to ask for free air conditioning and an upholstery upgrade. Who knows, he may just say yes. *Never* let a nibble go unanswered. Ask, Ask, Ask. No one will give you anything unless you ask for it.

TEMPORARY CONCESSIONS

Many times things that have been granted to you at earlier stages of negotiations disappear in financing—usually at about the time you start to feel good because you have almost bought a car. All those things you have fought so hard for sometimes get forgotten when you can smell the leather seats. To keep this from happening, *write down* all the agreed upon items and don't sign until you have everything you were promised. Get really upset if promises don't materialize. Concessions tend to disappear when the salesperson has promised you the moon and the person in financing knows nothing about it. Your best tactic here is to walk away quickly if they don't honor their commitments.

REFUSING TO NEGOTIATE

Some car companies, like the Saturn line or other car types that are in high demand, claim they don't negotiate. While they may not be flexible on new car price, they may give you a much higher trade-in, throw in extra accessories, or allow you a lower financing rate. Claiming not to negotiate is a great negotiating tactic or, at the very least, an interesting initial negotiating posture. Don't take them at their word. Even Saturn dealerships do sometimes negotiate on car price. In reality, a small percentage are sold below sticker price. My advice: keep probing for other concessions that effectively lower the price of the car, or shop elsewhere for a better deal.

QUOTING AVERAGES AND STATISTICS

Do long lists of facts, figures, and averages confuse you? If so, then block them out. Another way of dealing with your confusion is to profess complete ignorance, then move the conversation to a more comfortable topic. Here's an example:

SALES MANAGER (for the third time): ... and as you can see, you don't have to worry about price when you lease a car because the average cost of a Rule of 78 lease is much lower than even a conventional declining loan balance.

YOU: I still don't understand. What about color of upholstery? What choices do I have?

APPEALS TO YOUR SENSE OF FAIRNESS

Sellers are the only people who ever demand that you recognize their need to make money and get what they consider their due. It is Detroit's responsibility to price their cars correctly and to make profit for their dealerships and sales staff, not yours. Don't get sucked into this kind of debate. This is just a variation on the guilt tactic.

THE SILENT TREATMENT

When you notice that the salesperson has stopped talking and you begin to feel awkward, you are experiencing the silent treatment. This is your signal to start talking politics, baseball, or cooking. If that doesn't work, it is time to see how quiet he becomes when you walk out of the negotiating room into the parking lot towards your car. If silence makes you feel uneasy, don't stand for it.

"I'M NEW HERE"

Any good salesperson will attempt to make you his friend and elicit your sympathy. If he is really new, and naive, you can be sure that he has an experienced, strong, and competent sales manager backing him up. But who is going to intercede for you if you make a costly mistake based on his false information? Now is the time to take him at his word and to ask for someone more experienced. It's as simple as that.

THE GOOD FAITH DEPOSIT

Giving a deposit is perhaps one of the strongest signs of commitment. Don't do it unless you are prepared to really go through with the deal. If the salesperson will not take an offer to his boss without a check or deposit, demand that he do. Let him know that until a firm price is agreed on, you will not commit to the sale. If he refuses, threaten to walk. I guarantee he will chase you into the parking lot.

TAKING YOUR KEYS AND REGISTRATION

It is everybody's nightmare to have the dealer "lose" the keys to his car so he must stay and negotiate. Always bring an extra set of keys and don't negotiate until you get your keys and registration back.

"IF I CAN _____, WILL YOU _____?"

This is a great technique and is used all the time to get a buying commitment from the customer. This technique is designed to see if you are a real buyer, and perhaps to probe your limits. A typical example follows:

SALESPERSON: IF I CAN get the car in blue at your price, WILL YOU buy it right now?

or:

SALESPERSON: IF I CAN get my manager to buy your trade-in at your price, WILL YOU accept our price for the new car?

The best way to handle this tactic is to become a broken record. Keep restating your terms. If he gives you what you want, of course you will buy right then and there, if you want to. Later on, you can change your position if it suits you. After all, you can negotiate from limited authority as well as he can.

INTIMIDATION

At some point in the negotiations, usually an impasse, your salesperson will try to intimidate you by cheerfully inviting you to meet his manager. This is not like meeting the Queen of England. This is the real strong arm and he looks like he probably eats pit bull dogs for lunch. He also is pretty busy, so the best way to handle him is to delay, waffle, and then stick to your demands without being intimidated. The manager's job is to spend as much time as it takes to close the sale, so be prepared with some "killer" tactics.

STONEWALLING

Stonewalling, a classic negotiating position, is the granting of concessions slowly and grudgingly. The average person quickly becomes impatient and discouraged and compromises just to get the negotiations going. To beat this technique, you must be willing to outwait the salesperson, or to come in at a time that is so inconvenient that all he wants to do is get the transaction over with. This is why starting the buy one to two hours before closing will work well for you.

UPCOMING PRICE INCREASE

This is a scare tactic designed to get you to move really quickly. Typically, the salesperson tries to speed you towards making a decision by indicating that there is going to be a large price increase soon. Therefore you must buy this car now, because the price will be 6.8% or 10.2% or $500 more by the weekend.

The way to handle this is to ask the salesperson to document, through a bulletin or some other printed document, that there is going to be a price hike soon. Note the amount and the date it becomes effective and see if the price rise applies to your chosen car. Make sure that it does apply, because some price rises are not on all models.

If they can't produce documents, consider the statement as hot air, disregard it, and go on negotiating at your own speed. If it does apply, note it, and go on negotiating at your own speed.

Now that you are familiar with the car salesperson's arsenal of strategies, and how to counter them, let's see what powerful techniques are available to you.

Your Best Tactics

Giving you a list of counter tactics for each sales tactic won't work because you will lose if you try to play one-up on an experienced professional salesperson or sales manager. Not only will you lose, but you will be unable to achieve your primary goal — getting the best deal. You don't want to antagonize anyone; you just want them to give you their best deal. All of the following techniques are designed to achieve that end.

BROKEN RECORD

Of all the techniques in a car buyer's arsenal, the broken record tactic has got to be the best. It is used successfully by kids to grind down parents, by people with energy to wear down tired people, and by buyers with plenty of time to spend on car salespeople anxious to go home. Badly done, it is a transparent and annoying strategy. Combined with other techniques and done well, it can be subtle and very powerful.

Did you ever deal with a person who wouldn't budge from his point of view? Someone who just kept repeating himself endlessly, waiting for you to give in? If you are under time pressures, you usually give in just to get it over with. If you don't have to deal with broken record people, give them a wide berth. You see this technique used ad nauseam by groups like the National Rifle Association and the anti-gun groups when they confront each other. Each group just states and repeats its position. There is no real discussion — or progress.

In its simplest form, the broken record tactic is a constant restatement of your point of view. In its more refined form, it is a restatement of your position with a reasonable explanation added. Here is an example of the skillful use of the broken record tactic:

YOU: Yes, I know that you want to sell your car for $18,500 but I can only afford $16,500.

SALESPERSON: I would love to make a sale, but my boss just won't let me make a deal with almost no profit. You have to come up with more money, and maybe we can help you in terms of payments.

YOU: Yes, I know the deal is not great, but at $16,500 you will be making a good profit.

SALESPERSON: We are losing money at that price.

YOU: But you will make a decent profit, and if you look at my figures, you will see that $16,500 is fair. Other dealers are offering the same car at $16,000.

This cycle is repeated continually until a deal is reached or you (not they) leave. There is really no counter to this technique as long as it is done well. The technique is exceptionally powerful because there is no real way a salesperson can shut off or throw out a stubborn customer who may be a buyer and just keeps plugging away.

YES ... BUT ...

The buyer's main use of the YES ... BUT ... mechanism is to counter the salesperson's arguments without being obnoxious. Let's see how it is used in the following situation:

SALESPERSON: The list price for the car is $17,750 and at that price these cars are almost flying off the lot.

YOU: YES, I understand how you might want to get full price for your car, BUT I won't pay that much money.

This method of fighting for a price is much less confrontational than other methods.

FEEL/FELT/FOUND

Another version of the YES ... BUT ... tactic that is often used on you to diffuse a confrontation is the FEEL/FELT/FOUND technique. In the hands of an experienced salesperson it operates as follows:

YOU: I have heard from my friends that diesel engines are terrible.

SALESPERSON: I know how you FEEL (sales staff never disagree with you initially). I FELT the same way when I first got into this business, but I FOUND after I researched the subject that diesel engines make a lot of sense in circumstances like these.

Now that you see how this works, you will be able to use this technique on them:

SALESPERSON: Your offer is just too low, I can't take it to my boss.

YOU: I know that you FEEL my offer is low. My friends FELT the same way when I discussed the car buy with them, but I FOUND there was a lot of justification for my bid considering your cost structure and today's market.

YOU HAVE TO DO BETTER THAN THAT

Just saying, "You have to do better than that" is a great technique because it forces the salesperson to do something to rescue the sale. When you reach a deadlock, saying, "You will have to do better than that" forces her to do something. Sometimes the salesperson will make a concession without even knowing what it will take to save the situation. This technique works well when you neither you nor the salesperson will budge.

Here is an example of how to use this technique in combination with the broken record tactic.

YOU: You have to do better than that.

SALESPERSON: If I can get my boss to accept $300 less, will you buy a car right now, today?

YOU: I didn't make myself clear. You have to do considerably better than that and, yes, I really do want to buy a car today.

If the technique is used on you, the way to beat this technique is to ask exactly what is it you have to do better and get him to explain how much better and in what ways. Insist that he be specific, for example:

YOU: I want to pay $15,500 for the car.

SALESPERSON: You have to do better than that.

YOU: Tell me exactly what it is you need to make this deal go through.

SALESPERSON: I need more money.

YOU: Tell me exactly how far apart we are.

SALESPERSON: I know he won't let the car go for less than $17,200.

YOU: You will have to accept considerably less than that.

This combination of techniques is doubly powerful when used correctly.

WHY WON'T YOU LET ME BUY A CAR TODAY?

Asking, "Why won't you let me buy a car today?" is a technique designed to shock the salesperson. Usually, salespeople spend their time trying to get you, the customer, to make up your mind to buy a car. They think that the customer is the only one standing in the way of the sale. When you place the blame squarely on their shoulders, they are understandably confused. It is tremendously frustrating for them to try to explain why they won't let you get a car. When you use this technique, they will flounder around for a while before working their way out. Don't use it more than once. Its value is its initial impact as a shocker.

DELAY

Delay—especially if you arrived late in the day, it is the end of the month, and you are a real buyer. Usually customers get nervous because salespeople use delay as a tactic. However, at the end of the day, the sales staff wants to go home and no matter how cool they look, the longer you keep them late, the more they resent it and the more they speed up the whole negotiating process. Keeping them two hours over the end of their normal twelve-hour shift really tries their patience, especially if you are fresh and don't seem to be in a rush (and worse yet are a real customer). They can't kick you out. They don't want to kick you out. They just want to get the deal over with, even if they don't make as much as they would in another situation.

CHANGE OF PACE

In the usual car sale, the salesperson first closes on you for a commitment to buy a car and then he closes on you for a price. In the *ideal* sale, you should make up your mind to buy a car and then close on *him* for a better price. Change the pace.

This is a role reversal with the salesperson defending his position and you trying to find out what it will take for *him* to make a deal (the California technique reversed). Salespeople don't handle this well because they are put in a passive defensive position with a tough buyer who knows what is possible. My feeling is that you can get very close to the final figure if you have done your homework, know your prices, made yourself a real buyer, gone in late, and you are set to buy.

CREATE TENSION

Most people will do anything to reduce the tension in their lives. They are basically nice folks who get through life compromising and pleasing others. These are great people to marry or to have in a family, but they are not the right people to negotiate with a strong personality type. Car dealers handle these people by continually pushing them to the maximum. The salesperson constantly creates stress and forces the customer to find solutions to the problems they fabricate.

When you sense that you are being put under created tension, raise the tension level yourself. This is hard for most people to do, but the only other alternative is to give in. Here is a typical response to created tension:

SALESPERSON: I am sorry to say this, but your car is not worth $2250. My figure was only an estimate and my manager just told me this. I was pretty surprised that my used car manager will only give you $1200 for it. Can you come up with another $1000 so we can wrap up the new car?

YOU: I am really upset about this. You gave your word that the car was worth $2250. This is ridiculous, and I am going to terminate this discussion right now. Get me the sales manager; I want to complain. (You get up and start to leave.)

SALESPERSON: Wait a minute, wait a minute. (Suddenly scared, because he has obviously misjudged your reaction; he was hoping that you would easily accept the lower price.) Let me talk to him again, maybe I can get you a better price.

YOU: I will give you exactly five minutes to get this straightened out. Then I am leaving.

SALESPERSON: Let me take care of this right away — I assure you it won't happen again. (He knows that he will have to treat you with kid gloves from now on!)

When someone has to reduce the tension level, let it be the dealership, not you.

SAY NO ONE MORE TIME

When you get to a point where you are almost in agreement and the sales manager (you are long past the salesperson) offers to split the difference, don't do anything right away. Don't look happy; don't look anxious; just say no one more time and see what happens. No matter how pleased you are with the agreement, make yourself say no one more time just to see what else falls in your plate (even if doing so makes you uncomfortable).

Now that you have read enough to know what tactics you can use and how powerful they can be in the hands of an informed consumer, you are probably rerunning your last car buy in your mind and kicking yourself because of all the things you did wrong. If only you knew then what you know now.

Now let's take a critical look at what probably happened to you last time with an eye toward avoiding a repeat next time.

13

Examples of
Bad Negotiating

IS THIS WHAT HAPPENED LAST TIME?

Most people don't remember the details of their last car buy. All they know is they ended up with higher payments than they expected. Some people don't even know what their car really cost them. All they know is that it wasn't paid off when they were ready to sell it. I've heard so many car war stories and been to so many dealerships that I've decided to show you how it happens.

As you drive your mud-spattered old car into the lot of a local new car dealership, it backfires, thus alerting the sales staff that you have arrived. You, your spouse, and three kids get out. You are tired after a twelve-hour shift and are still wearing your work clothes. As you enter the showroom, a salesperson comes forward to greet you.

YOU: Can you show me some cars?

Your body language tells the salesperson that you are really tired and are doing this after work. Your clothing indicates that in spite of your immediate need for a car, you may not be able to afford one. Your car looks as though it may not make it out of the lot, and your frazzled-looking spouse and kids indicate that you want to get this over with as quickly as possible.

The salesperson is thinking, "These people may be a credit risk. I bet their credit report is really marginal. At least they could have spiffed up the trade-in. With the whole family here, they will probably agree to almost anything. If they give me a hard time I will blow them off. But if they do buy, they will definitely pay full price."

FRIENDLY SALESPERSON (FSP): Hi, I'm Joe Carshark, how do you like these cars? They are the best to come out of Detroit in years. I am really glad you came today because this is our once a year founder's sale and we have been doing so well that we only have a few models left in stock. We are going to put you in the seat of the car of your dreams right now. Are you ready to buy a car today?

YOU: Slow down, slow down. I haven't even decided what model I want yet. I like to take my time and not be pressured. I've had a long day. I just came in for a test drive and to ask a few questions.

PROBLEM: All you have done here is to indicate to your FSP that you are irritable, can't stand pressure, and may not be a serious buyer. These kinds of statements at the beginning don't buy you credibility or a better deal. There is plenty of time to show him who is boss later on. If anything, it's smart strategy to be easy and enthusiastic initially, and hard later on.

FSP: I understand how you feel about pressure. A lot of people feel the same way you do about buying a car. But people who come to this dealership have complimented us on our friendly, civilized approach. We realize that buying a car is stressful and we plan to make the whole experience as easy for you as possible. We even have some toys for the kids. By the way, I also hate salespeople, especially insurance salespeople. You don't sell insurance, do you? Ha ha. (The salesperson is using the feel/felt/found technique to defuse your resentment. He is also trying to qualify you as a real buyer by probing your financial situation.)

YOU: No, actually I work at Consolidated Aircraft. I'm a junior engineer and have been working part time for a few months now, but I hope to be called back to full-time work soon. Probably in two to three weeks at the most.

PROBLEM: Bad, bad, bad. The FSP now knows that you are practically unemployed and may not be able to afford a new car. This means higher interest rates, a higher down payment, and more pressure on you to prove that you qualify for credit. In addition, now he'll have less patience with you if you prove to be a difficult buyer. In general, do not divulge any personal information. Remember the "Miranda Warning" from earlier in the book; everything your FSP finds out now "can and will be used against you."

FSP: Yes, I've heard that times are tough, but with our special incentives and rebates we're seeing a lot of action. Speaking of action, did you see the Cowboys (or the Raiders or the Cubs or whatever the local favorite team is) last weekend? (The FSP is now trying to become your friend, because people buy more easily from people they like and trust. He has pegged you as an amiable person who needs to establish a personal relationship with someone before they buy.)

YOU: Well, I'm actually not a Cowboys fan, I like the Giants.

FSP: Yes, me too! They are having a great year this year. (You can bet he will like whatever you like whether it be football, politics, polo, or collecting bottle openers. At this point, your FSP is concentrating on defusing your earlier perceptions about salespeople and trying to find out what emotional buttons to push.)

FSP: What kind of car were you considering?

YOU: I need a station wagon, and I don't want to pay more than $17,000. I can afford monthly payments of $400 or so a month.

PROBLEM: As soon as you mention price and payments, the FSP thinks that you will be willing to pay *at least* $17,000 and *at least* $400 a month, probably more. Since you weren't shy about mentioning money — a delicate subject for most customers, the FSP feels he can get as much information out of you as he needs. He is encouraged and immediately launches into his pitch.

FSP: Before we go on, tell me, did you see our ad, or hear about us from a friend?

YOU: Well, my dad always had good luck with your cars, my old car is about dead, and the whole family hates it (spouse nods obviously and emphatically). We want a new car now.

PROBLEM: Bad, bad, you've just told your FSP where all your hot buttons are. You *need*, not *want*, a car now and you know your trade-in isn't worth much. So the FSP will feel free to give you a low price for your trade-in. You also told him that pleasing your family is a factor in this buy. They are pushing for a new car. He will load you with lots of options — that means extra profit for the dealership. Now that he has this valuable information, he will hold out the carrot of the test drive while he probes for more information.

FSP: Well, know that I know where you stand, let's go for a test drive. What sort of equipment do you want on your new car?

YOU: I really don't want much more than a bare bones car, but my spouse wants power everything.

FSP: I can understand that. Some people like every comfort in a car. By the way, before we take the test drive, do you plan to buy the car for cash, or are you going to finance through us? Also, what about the down payment?

YOU: We have enough cash for a good down payment, but the monthly payments will be a problem.

PROBLEM: You have just qualified yourself as a payment buyer, so later complaints that the car costs too much will be ignored and countered with talk of better payments or a larger down payment. Also, since payments are your big issue, he will not worry about giving you much for your trade-in.

FSP: Trust me. If you can come up with a good down payment, we can get you really good monthly payments.

PROBLEM: He has already decided that you sure aren't going to get that down payment from your trade-in. Also, those "really good monthly payments" will be spread out for seventy-two months, or six years!

YOU: Boy, that's a relief! I was really afraid of high payments. Let's do take that test drive.

FSP: Fine, but just to save time later, fill out this credit application before we go for a test drive. That way we can do a credit check on you and have all the information by the time we get back.

YOU: No problem. (But you are wondering what your credit report really says; you haven't checked it recently. This is the beginning of a panic attack.)

Finally, your FSP takes you all out for a drive in an upscale model with all the extras including a bigger motor so you will be safer getting onto the expressways. When you question the cost of all these extras, he assures you that they are easily within your price range.

During the test drive, the FSP continually probes and endeavors to discover (and answer) any objections you might have. He makes comments like, "Do you like this type of upholstery?" or "We have an upgrade sound system available," or "By the way, did you notice the pinstriping as you got in? We have a special deal on it this month."

After the test drive, you and your FSP take a look at your old car. As he walks around it, he doesn't say anything, but he taps on parts of the car that are dented, stained, or imperfect. He fingers rips in the upholstery, and makes sure that you know that he hears noises in the engine. Each time he discovers a "defect" that you knew was there but had sort of grown used to, your heart stops and your hope of getting a good trade-in price further decreases. He won't directly say the car is bad; but the FSP lets you infer it from his actions.

FSP: Let's go inside now. I'll have our used car manager really go over your car. It's really not my department, so I can't quote you a price. I just hope he feels it is worth more than I do. Hopefully, he will let us use it as a trade-in. But I have to warn you he is a really difficult person. He may not want this vehicle at all (at this point he notes the panicked look in your eye) but I can handle him. By the way, have you ever considered selling this car yourself?

YOU: No, I haven't. I hate writing ads and staying home all weekend. Besides, I'm a terrible salesperson; I just can't stand haggling with people.

FSP now knows what you will do if you are offered a low price on your trade-in. You have left yourself no options. You will not sell the car yourself, and you have admitted that you do not like to argue or haggle. At this point the FSP is setting the stage for hooking you into the new car first, *then* confirming what you already know — that your used car isn't worth much.

FSP: Now let's really talk turkey. It's obvious that you like the car with all the extras; the bigger engine, the sun roof, the upgrade upholstery, don't you? (This is a technique: he is making a statement and getting you to agree to it by asking you a question which has only one answer — yes.)

YOU: Sure, I mean, what's not to like? But I'm not sure if we can afford it. I already told you how much I can afford to pay monthly. Is it within that range?

FSP: You quoted me a figure of $400/month, but that was for a bare bones car. If you can go just a little higher, to $450, and put down about $3000 we can put you in the driver's seat right now. What do you say? (A big silence here. Soon both you and your spouse both nod; this is called a silent close and is very powerful.)

Notice that he has gotten you to forget about the price of the car. Now, all he will talk about from this point on is payments.

FSP: Think of it this way. It isn't what you pay for the car, it's your monthly payments that are important, don't you agree? (Another big silence here, and you both nod in agreement.)

FSP: Since you both like the car and can afford the payments, let's do the paperwork right now. Okay?

YOU: I guess so.

PROBLEM: At this point you have essentially agreed to buy a car today, and if there is a later problem, FSP will remind you of this. Remember he negotiates from limited authority, he can say, "My boss won't let me do that." But if you agree to something and then back away, he will accuse you of being dishonest or not playing fair, etc.

SPOUSE: I agree that the payments are important. We really do love the car, but I think we should backtrack a little. What about our trade-in? It really is a nice car.

YOU: (You vividly remember the friendly salesperson noticing all the defects in the car.) Well, honey, let's not go overboard. You know it has dents and it doesn't start real well. (To FSP): Has your manager decided what he'll give us for the car?

At this point your salesperson excuses himself to find out, leaving you alone to worry for what seems like an hour. Finally, he returns:

FSP: I have bad news. Our used car manager feels it is only worth about $500 to $600 dollars at best. It's not really the kind of vehicle we usually even keep on our lot. Look, let's sit down and talk about the new car first and then handle the trade. It might take me some time to convince him, but as soon as we're done here I'll try again. Maybe I can get you a better allowance.

YOU: Please tell him that it's in good shape for a six year-old car. It starts a little hard in cold weather, but otherwise it's a great little car.

PROBLEM: The FSP thinks his position is solid because you have accepted him as your advocate. He takes strong control now

FSP: If we do take your trade-in for $600 with your $3500 cash down — it was $3500 you were going to put down in cash wasn't it? (You nod yes even though you really don't remember.) If you can give me, say $475 a month, we can work out a deal.

The conversation will go on and on like this with you giving in a little and him waffling, until a final monthly payment (not a car *price*) is agreed upon.

Several times during the negotiation, another person will wander into the room and speak to you and your FSP. This person will say things like, "Let's finish things up here as soon as possible, if you can. It's already an hour after closing time and we've been keeping the financing staff waiting," or, "I just want to let you know that I just got a chance to speak with the manager about your trade-in and we're giving you top dollar. He says we'll probably have to junk it, so I just want to let you know that we're doing all we can."

In most dealerships, the *closer* is the real salesperson. He is the person the dealership depends on not to let the customer get away. Your FSP assures you that he has everything under control and tells you not to worry about the closer.

Sometime later, after giving up and agreeing to whatever it is you have agreed to, you will go for a chat with the finance person, who will dismiss your FSP and usher you into his office. Even though you are thinking that you really need a break here (by this time you're really tired and a bit confused), you are also anxious to finish the deal and get home, so you don't protest.

FINANCE PERSON: You people really look beat, but don't worry, it's almost over. I'm as anxious as you are to get this over with so I can hand you the keys to your new car. It is a beauty, isn't it? (He then stops and waits for an answer.)

YOU: Yes, we just love the car, but can we afford it?

SPOUSE: We really do want this car. We haven't spent all this time here for nothing. It's getting late and the children have to get to bed.

YOU: What do we have to do to get it now?

FINANCE PERSON: Well, we do have a little problem with your credit report. You do know that, don't you?

YOU: Well, I did have some problems three years ago, but I am in pretty good shape now. That old problem wasn't supposed to be on my record.

That was some time ago, and I am making regular payments now. Does this mean you can't get me financed?

FINANCE PERSON: Don't worry; we will figure it out somehow, I know that we are going to have trouble getting you the low interest rate we promised. That is only for people with *good* credit. Lucky for you, we are a large dealership and have been in business for years. We have special credit sources available to help you. You may have to pay an extra point or two, but I can't see any other way of obtaining the financing. You do understand, don't you? (Nice guilt attack and a little bit of "I am the good guy" routine. You now feel so unsure of yourself that you probably will not even contest the higher interest rate that will be artfully buried in the finance charges.)

YOU: Well, we certainly appreciate your help. (Like most people who have had credit problems, you feel guilty and fully expect that most institutions will not lend you money. So the friendly person helping you now seems like your only hope.)

FINANCE PERSON: Come to think of it, I do have another suggestion that might help you. Do you have any other sources of money? Instead of $3500 down if you can come up with about $1000 more we can probably keep the interest rate lower, say only two or three points higher than conventional. I would like to be able to do that for you.

YOU: I guess I can come up with some more down money as long as the payments are still within the $450/month we agreed on.

FINANCE PERSON: Also, I would like you to consider getting our extended seven-year guarantee on the engine and drive train. It only costs $995—and it's a guarantee you really can't afford to be without. The engine and drive train are the most expensive parts of the car and our guarantee protects you.

YOU: I really can't afford it.

FINANCE PERSON: We can finance the cost and just add it in your monthly payments; you'll never even notice it.

YOU: Well, yes. But it seems like a lot of money.

FINANCE PERSON: If we can finance it for $20 a payment can we just add it in? You do want it, don't you?

YOU: Well, yes. If we can finance it. But …

FINANCE PERSON: (interrupting) What about an anti-theft protection system? (Here he goes on to a new topic and thus assumes an agreement in the absence of an objection.) And what about a protective coating for the outside of the car as well?

YOU: How much more is that?

FINANCE PERSON: Oh, about $18 a month.

YOU: I don't want it.

SPOUSE: I think we should definitely get the anti-theft system. After all I work at night and some of those neighborhoods are pretty bad.

YOU: Okay, okay. But I really don't want anything else.

From the tone of your voice, a good finance person knows that it is time to stop. He has pushed you to the limit. To push you further might endanger the sale. So he ushers you to a waiting room and offers you some drinks and donuts. He says he needs a few minutes to prepare the paperwork and make some phone calls. The mention of phone calls worries you and as you wait, your anxiety level rises as you anticipate additional complications.

Fifty long minutes later he comes back in saying he has finally put together something which may work but you will have to pay three points over conventional loan rates — your credit was worse than you thought and the bank has to be protected. You give in with a sense of relief. He pushes the stack of contracts over for you to sign. You do, glad that your ordeal is finally over.

As you drive out in your new car, your family regards you as a hero. But all their excitement and happiness can't keep you from feeling bad. You chalk it up to tiredness, but the real truth is:

- You put down more money than you had intended (a lot more money).
- You paid a higher interest rate than you had intended.
- You got practically nothing for your trade-in.
- You paid top dollar for your new car.
- You didn't get the bare bones model you wanted.
- You really don't know the exact cost of the car.

Don't let this happen to you — ever again.

14

Effective Negotiating Dialogues

HOW TO NEGOTIATE WELL

In the last chapter you saw how negotiating should not go. Perhaps you even saw what happened to you on your last car-buying excursion. Now, let's see how it should go if you do it correctly.

We will use the same cast of characters with one addition: the feared sales manager, also called the closer. In most dealerships, the closer is the person the dealership depends on not to let customers get away. This is the person with the authority to make a deal, the boss. This is the person who must make sure the dealership doesn't give away the store on new or used car prices and make sure the dealership earns a good return on its cars. This person has come up through the ranks and is cunning, experienced, knowledgeable, and of the right mental attitude to do a good job. This person earns a good living by producing a lot of sales at high profit margins. This is the real bad guy.

So just how do you deal with everything above plus this new person? Consider the following scenario, I hope it will give you a good idea of how to apply everything you have read so far in this book. Make this buyer your model and you will fare very well in your next car buy:

You arrive at the lot, your four-year-old car fairly gleaming with the polish job you have given it. The black wall tires are really black. There is no dust or dirt on the car and it looks far better than the used cars already on the lot. (During the negotiations, you see used car customers looking at your car.) You get out. If you feel you are a competent buyer, you may have come alone, more than likely you have some support with you, but you surely don't have crying children, or anything else that won't help you.

You are well dressed, well rested, lightly fed, and have all night to buy a car. You have done your homework and have the results with you and committed to memory. You also have priced your trade-in and know its approximate worth. You have obtained outside financing that you are prepared to use if you have to. At this point you are ready to deal and are not afraid of any salesperson who has ever lived. You would like to buy a car today, but can wait until next week or even next month if necessary.

The date is within the last three days of the month, the time is one to two hours before the dealership's closing time. (If everything is perfect, it is Christmas Eve, there is a snowstorm, and the salespeople all have the flu. But, what the heck, you can't have everything.)

YOU: If I can find the kind of car I want, I would like to buy a car today. Do you understand? I really want to buy a car today.

FRIENDLY SALESPERSON (FSP) thinks your body language, your clothes, and the condition of your trade-in all indicate that you are capable of affording a new car and are probably a good prospect to buy one today. As today hasn't been a really good day for anyone in the dealership, he is already anxious to make this sale work.

FSP: Hi, I am your friendly salesperson and I would love to sell you a car today. And let me tell you, we have some great cars and we are willing to deal. What type of car are you interested in?

YOU: Can you show me your full-sized sedan? Oh, I would also like to look at your station wagon model. By the way, I know it is late. Will the dealership stay open long enough for us to talk and make a deal today or should I come back next week?

FSP: We will absolutely stay open until we conclude our business. No question about that. By the way, good choice, these are some of the best-selling models in the good old USA.

NOTE: He has just committed himself to staying as late as you want. This makes it tough for him complain about how long it is taking to make a deal, how late it is, or how badly he wants to go home. Also don't think that these people don't notice everything about you or your trade-in as they try to figure out what is going on in your life and mind and how best to control you.

FSP: I see from your parking sticker that you work for Consolidated Aircraft.

YOU: Yes, great company. Been there seven years. We are really going to beat this recession with the new products that will be coming out soon. (No need to tell the FSP that you haven't worked full-time for several months, just act upbeat. The fact that you are buying a car while practically out of work is none of his business, so don't tell him. This is not an endorsement to buy a car while on layoff, but an indication of how to handle a difficult situation.)

FSP will now show you things about the car and will take you on a test drive. Meanwhile, he will be asking you questions about how you like the car and if you can afford it. He is pre-qualifying you.

Before you go on the test drive, toss the salesperson the keys to your trade-in and say, "I am serious about buying one of these cars, but to save time, have your used car manager look at my trade-in so he can give me a price when we come back from the test drive."

FSP: The used car manager usually likes to have the seller of the car with him when he goes over the car. We also need to have a credit check done. Can you fill out a credit application so we can qualify you?

YOU: It's late now and I don't care to go over my car with him. I know its condition and if he is a professional, he will know it also. Let me give you one of my credit card numbers so that you can check my credit, and I will gladly fill out an application now or can do so when we get back. Is that satisfactory?

NOTE: Do not be around when they evaluate your car. They will spend most of their time trying to devalue it in your eyes. They will also fish around for you to commit to the lowest price you will accept for it. Let them guess without you. There is no advantage for you in being with them. The credit qualification is legitimate. Make it easy for them to get the information. It makes you more of a real buyer.

The FSP then takes you for a test drive.

FSP: Isn't the ride great on this car?

YOU: It's nice.

FSP: Isn't the engine quiet?

YOU: It's fine.

FSP: Isn't the interior roomy? (etc.)

YOU: Sure is.

NOTE: The trick here is to indicate to the salesperson that the car is adequate and that if the price is right, you may buy it. Don't gush all over about how great the car is. Don't be too critical unless you plan not to buy the car. The neutral attitude will leave you with the most negotiating latitude. Be pleasant, non-critical, and unemotional. Give few buying signals.

FSP: I hope you like the car as much as I do and that you will buy one because there are only a few of this type left and you don't want to miss out on a great car. (The going going gone tactic. In my way of thinking, when a salesperson starts the battle and uses one recognizable technique it is morally okay for us buyers to do what we must to counter the offensive.)

YOU: I understand that I may not get the car, but I can live with that. I am certain that you have others I may be interested in. (This is the counter to going going gone.)

The FSP may also try variations on this theme such as:

FSP: That lady over there is interested in this car and if you don't hurry up and buy it, she may get it first.

YOU: If it happens, it happens. But you do understand that I really want to buy a car today, don't you?

NOTE: It is in a salesperson's job description to find out how you feel about the car and to determine how best to hook you. He will try to create a need for *immediate* action in you. You can neutralize him by continually indicating that you want to buy a car today *if* everything goes right.

This is the time for you to ask him about details of the car that bother you. If the suspension is too soft, ask if you can get an upgrade in suspension. Some of these people know the cars they are selling and can handle questions you may have from your readings.

FSP: Shall we go into the showroom and put some numbers down on paper and see if you can afford this beauty? (This is where he sees if you are really serious.)

YOU: Absolutely, but first I want to see the price you are going to give me for my used car. I feel I should tell you that this price is very important to me. If I can get a good price on my trade-in, the rest of this transaction should proceed quickly. If I cannot get what I consider is an adequate price I will walk immediately. I do not expect to have my intelligence insulted. You do understand that, don't you?

FSP: I will get the sales manager's figure as soon as we go inside. But let me warn you, he is a tough person to get a high price out of.

YOU: Yes, I understand that you have to make a profit, but I must get my price for the car or I can't go any further with this transaction, and I really want to buy a car today. Do you understand that? (Notice the yes ... but tactic.)

FSP: I will do my best for you. What sort of price did you want for your trade-in?

YOU: Let's go inside, get the figure from your used car manager, and see if it meets what I need.

FSP: Yes, but what kind of figure do you need?

YOU (playing broken record): Let's go inside and get the figure from the used car manager and see what it is first. Do you understand that if the figure is too far off we may have trouble making a deal?

NOTE: This speech is designed to prevent him from lowballing you on your trade-in price. Do not name a figure. Wait and see what they offer first.

Go into the negotiating room, but don't do anything substantial until the price of the trade-in comes back. Many dealerships prefer to sell you a new car first and then to give you a price on your trade-in later after you are committed to the nice new car.

FSP: My manager is looking at the car and will have a bid for you in a few minutes. In the meantime, why don't you tell me if you like the car? We can discuss price, options, and other details while we wait.

YOU (now is the time to show him who is boss): I would love to discuss these items, but I feel that I can't do much else until my mind is clear about how much I am going to get for my trade-in. Then I can plan the amount I will pay for the new car and other such things.

FSP: Why don't we start now and let the trade-in price catch up with us? I'm sure it will be here soon. By the way, if the real problem is payments, I am sure we can get you very low payments. Let's look at leasing; we can get you super low payments by leasing. Incidentally, have you paid off your car, if not we can tie the payoff into your new lease payments. Would you like to lease?

NOTE: He is now trying to close the sale on a minor point, which then assumes that you have closed on the major points of the sale itself *and* the car's price — sticker price at this point.

YOU: Yes, I have paid off my car. Payments are not the problem, and I prefer not to discuss them now. I hope that the trade-in price comes soon and is reasonable, otherwise I am just wasting my time and may not be able to conclude this negotiation tonight.

FSP: Well, we definitely want to put you in the seat of the car you want and we want to do it tonight. Let me go see our used car manager and push him along … Oh, one more point, if I get you a good allowance on your trade-in towards an upgrade model of the sedan with all the bells and whistles you wanted, would you consider buying it tonight, right away?

YOU: I am not interested in talking about allowances or payments. Let's just find out what price you are going to give me on my trade-in and then we can see what kind of price you can give me on the sedan. It is too early to talk financing or those sort of issues.

FSP: Okay, I'll be back in a minute with the trade-in price. (Under his breath "This is one tough customer; it is going to be hard to switch and confuse this one.")

NOTE: He tried to confuse you with payments, then he tried to confuse the issue with allowances, and he tried to get a new car decided on before giving a price on the trade-in. He wants you to commit to the new car and this in itself will devalue your trade-in. He tried and failed to get a commitment to buy this car tonight under any circumstances.

FSP returns with a number that is below the auction price for the car. You know this because you have done all of your homework and know what your car would go for at auction.

YOU: I indicated that the trade-in price for this car was important to me, and yet you come back with a figure that is not only below retail and wholesale, but below *auction value* as well. I am very disappointed. Let me say this one more time — the trade-in price for the car is of paramount value to me. I need a price near to Blue Book wholesale for the car in order to continue this sale. If we can work this out, I'm sure that the rest of the transaction will go smoothly. I really do want to buy a car today, do you understand?

FSP: This is the price he gave me, but let me go back and talk to him in a little while and see what I can do. In the meantime, let's talk about the price of the new car.

YOU: Let's settle the trade-in first. I have made myself as clear as I possibly can. I need about Blue Book wholesale in order to go on with this negotiation. If you can't get near it, tell me now and you can save us both a lot of time and energy by cutting this discussion short. I won't discuss a new car until this issue is settled.

NOTE: For the FSP, this is a worst case scenario. He knows now that he must eventually come within $200 of your asking price and hope to make his money elsewhere in the transaction.

After the trade-in price is finally settled, the FSP tries to move the negotiation along.

FSP: Now that we have the trade-in price settled, and you know that I got you the best price I could for your car, let's deal on this beautiful new car you picked out. You do love it, don't you?

YOU: The car is great, but first let's talk about what equipment is on the car, what the guarantees are, and what upgrades make sense to give me the performance I want. Then we can talk new car price. By the way, I have written down the figure you gave me for the trade-in. This is correct, isn't it?

FSP: Yes, that is correct, and you must admit it is a good price.

YOU: Yes, it allows us to go on with our discussion.

Some time later, the technical details have been established and you have either decided on a car with all of the features you want, ordered a car from the factory, or settled for what he has on his lot at this time.

FSP: Now that we have decided on all the details, how much do you want to buy the car for? I can get you really great payments.

YOU: I know you aren't going to like the price I am going to mention, but if we can agree on it, I will buy this car today. This new car price is the most important item left to discuss. By the way, it is important to me that we settle on a price and discuss payments later.

NOTE: You tied down the trade-in price by having him acknowledge it. Now you are going to shock him with a figure for his new car that is just barely within the acceptable range. You will not talk allowances or financing, just new car price in dollars.

YOU: I know you have to make a profit, but it is going to be a small one. I am going to give you $17,300 for this car. This will include all the present equipment on the car and transportation. I have calculated what your costs for this car and I know that my price allows you $300 profit. You will notice I have not included any of the items listed on the extra sticker including the ADMU (additional dealers markup), the cost for the rustproofing that you haven't put on yet, and the stain protection on the upholstery.

FSP winces as you mention the price. (All good sales staff wince or jump or make some involuntary gesture when you mention a price. It gives the impression that the price is ridiculous.)

FSP: That's too low. Our sticker for this car is $20,436 even dropping the ADMU, which is put on all hot cars — and this car is *hot*. I might manage to give you a $500 discount and even drop the ADMU for a serious customer. This would get the price down to $19,436 — if I can get it by our sales manager. By the way, you probably know that the manufacturer is giving rebates of $750, so this price would be really close to what you want.

YOU: Yes, I understand that you might want more for your vehicle, but times are tough and all I want to spend is $17,300 for the car as it is. Of course, the tax and licensing are separate issues, as are the rebates. I expect to get them regardless.

NOTE: Keep the discussion focused on your price. Play yes … but … and broken record with him. Occasionally give a few dollars away and try to settle for $400-500 (if the car is really in demand) or less over his cost. With a hot car you will pay more; with a slow seller, less. Walk out if you must, but if it is late in the evening and after closing time, he will eventually settle for what he can. Be patient, wait him out, be insistent. You should realize, of course, that a super hot car (like the Miata in 1989) may go for list or even above!

FSP: I can't give you your price without giving you a smaller allowance on your trade-in.

YOU: Excuse me; I thought we had that settled. You have already acknowledged that the trade-in price is a *fixed firm price*. It is definitely not an allowance. If this causes a problem with you, let's stop where we are and renegotiate the trade-in price. By the way it looks like we aren't going to finish by closing time: is that a problem? I really want to buy a car today.

to finish by closing time: is that a problem? I really want to buy a car today.

NOTE: *Don't let him change the trade-in price.* Don't let him call it an allowance. Stick to the new car price and tell him repeatedly that you want to buy a car today. He will try lots of these tricks.

Keep this line of discussion up. Be sure not to give much away. Never discuss the list price for the car, keep the discussion on your offered price; the list price is irrelevant and you should not hesitate to tell him that you know that. Don't let him switch you to another car or work in an allowance. Stick to price only. Threaten to walk out. Ask to see his boss. Waste his time and make it clear that you are in no hurry to leave. Remind him that you are a real buyer. Close on him for a price.

Some time later, you will have finally settled on a fixed firm price for the new car.

FSP: You got a really good price, but I guess you knew that. Let's put you in with our finance person and see what we can do to help you afford the car. By the way, we are having a special on alarm systems, and the outside protection package we put on the car is the best available.

YOU: Thanks for the help. You were a very helpful and professional salesperson and I will pass on your competence to your boss when I meet him. I do appreciate your efforts. I will take up the optional items with your finance person. By the way, I need to take a break for a few minutes. Is it possible for me to have a cup of coffee alone to think about the sale?

FSP will show you the waiting area and will nervously leave you alone. After you have taken a fifteen-minute break, gotten some coffee under your belt, you feel ready for dealing with the finance person. The time now is at least an hour after closing and everybody wants to go home but you. The salesperson, sales manager, finance person, and all the other people who are waiting around for you to finish up all want to go home. You may be anxious, but so are they, and they are tired after a twelve- to fourteen-hour day. If they press you, turn the pressure back on them by becoming somewhat unpredictable. Don't be rude or abrasive; it doesn't pay. But remember that your power is almost at its greatest now and you do not have take any garbage from anyone.

FINANCE PERSON: I know you are worried about not being able to afford this new car, but I am sure we can get you really great financing so your monthly payments are low. But first, have you considered getting our outside care package, normally it costs $600, but is on special this week only for $375, and ...

YOU (interrupting): I don't want any of those items you mentioned at any price, including the insurance. But if you can get the price of the extended warranty down from $995 to something reasonable I might consider it. Give me your best figure on it or else drop the subject. Also

I am not worried about the loan. I already have one at an amount large enough to cover the new car at 12.75% from my credit union. Can you beat it?

FINANCE PERSON: I can get you down to $895 on the extended warranty, but we have so little profit on this deal that you have to let us make a profit on some of these other items. I mean it's only fair that we make some money, right?

YOU: I hope you make enough money on the next deal to live long and prosper, but if that is the best you can do on the extended warranty, let's pass for now. What is the best you can do on the interest rate? Let's discuss monthly payments later. Can you beat 12.75%?

FINANCE PERSON: We have a special with our bank and I know we can get you lower rates and a lower payment. Tell you what, if you pick up the exterior care package for $350, I will get you an interest rate of 12.25 which will pay for the car care package over the lifetime of the car. So, not only will I get you a cheaper interest rate, but you will have the car care package for free! Doesn't that sound great?

YOU: Your loan is Rule of 78 isn't it? (See Chapter 16 for more about the "Rule of 78.")

FINANCE PERSON (amazed that you have even heard of Rule of 78): Of course, every loan in the business is.

YOU: Well my loan from my credit union is simple interest on the declining balance. If yours is Rule of 78, I will need more than a half point off the interest rate. If you can get me 11.75% I would consider it. Oh, if you can get me the extended warranty for $500, I might consider it also.

NOTE: The negotiations will now go back and forth, and the finance person and you will eventually reach an agreement that you both can live with. But you will not give back anything on the trade-in, or the new car price, and you will not be scared of losing the new car because of financing problems — you have a loan already, so what can he threaten you with? All you do will be to buy the best items at the best price and nothing else. After you agree on interest rate, then you specify the number of months and check his figure against the figure you got from the bank or looked up yourself in the book of interest payments.

OVERVIEW: At this stage, two or three hours after closing, everyone wants to go home, so there is less pressure on you, but more on the finance person. If he drops the ball, everybody has stayed overtime for nothing. You are essentially home free and he is under the gun. The next step is to utilize the information in the next chapter about things to ask, things to sign, and self checks to make sure you are not taken for a ride. You have a good buy almost under your belt: don't drop the ball yet.

15

Leasing

After the trade-in price has been settled, the decision to buy made, the price decided on, and the extras determined comes the job of deciding how to pay. To buy or to lease becomes the question. In many cases, it is unclear which is better. The rule is that leasing makes sense if you are short on down payment and/or you need low monthly payments.

PROS AND CONS OF LEASING

Leasing is great because your down payments are usually lower and your monthly payments are considerably lower. However, leasing also has a darker side.

♦ At the end of the contract you don't own the car.

♦ There are usually a lot of turn-in fees payable at the end of the lease.

♦ You may also not know what you paid for the new vehicle, the used vehicle, or anything else; just the payment amount per month and the number of months you are to make the payments.

♦ Manufacturers and dealers love leasing because more people can afford the monthly payments and at the lease end, they are back in the market for another car. If manufacturers and dealers love something, you should immediately be wary of it.

♦ Leases customarily run for three years. At the end of that time you will be looking for a new car (or lease).

♦ The idea of leasing is so good people may not even fight for a good buy; they just roll over.

♦ Leasing is so complex that more profit can be hidden in the leasing structure.

If you decide to lease, be aware of your motivation. Don't use leasing just to get low payments after you have failed to get a good enough price on the vehicle. Fight hard for a good trade-in, a great price on the new car, and everything else outlined above, and *then* negotiate hard for the best leasing terms.

LEASING CONSIDERATIONS

Following is a list of items to discuss before getting into the complicated topic of leases.

Initial Considerations

♦ Do you want a closed or open lease? The car will have a fixed or a non-fixed value at completion of the lease. In a closed lease, the leased car has a fixed price at the completion of the lease. Most leases now are closed end. The advantage of a closed end lease is that there are no surprises at the end of the lease period.

♦ Do you want to keep the car after the end of the lease?

♦ How much security deposit do they want? Try to keep it to a minimum. A security deposit, usually refundable, protects the bank or leasing company from excessive wear and tear. A security deposit is typically one month's payment. Try not to let it exceed that amount. The best argument to give them is that you don't want to pay this fee at all because you are a neat, careful, and conscientious individual who will take great care of the car.

Price Determining Items

♦ Price for the car. Did you negotiate the best price for the car? How close was it to the dealer's cost? (Remember, you do not want to pay over $300-400 above dealer's cost.)

♦ Price for your trade-in. How close was it to Blue Book wholesale? (Remember, your goal is to get within $200 of Blue Book wholesale for your trade-in.)

♦ Did you pay for an ADMU, AMU, dealer advertising, or dealer prep (cleaning up and maintaining the vehicle)?

♦ Is there factory cash back to be used towards the car? How much? While factory-to-consumer rebates are usually advertised, factory-to-dealer incentives are not. Ask the dealer directly if he is getting any factor-to-dealer rebates. Demand an answer. Don't let him put you off by telling you that it is none of your business. If he won't give you a figure, estimate it at a level that is to his disadvantage. For instance, if he refuses to tell you anything, say, "Well then, I will assume that you are being given $1,000 from the factory for each of these you sell. Therefore, I will expect the price to be considerably lower." This will usually force an answer. Insist that it is critical to the sale that you know the answer to this question.

♦ What kind of options did you pay for? Did you take any options that you did not want?

♦ How much do you have to finance? _____ (This is called your acquisition price. You figure it by subtracting your trade-in price, rebates, and discounts on equipment packages from the best car price. Make sure that you write that acquisition price down as a number.

Interest

♦ What is the dealership's interest rate for leasing?
♦ How does it compare to a bank's interest rate?
♦ How long do you want to lease for?

Points to Argue

♦ What residual value is the dealership going to give you? (The residual value is the car's value after the lease is over.) Try negotiating it upward. If it isn't reasonable, have them look at another leasing institution to get a higher value. One way to see if the residual value is reasonable is to compare the depreciation percentages of previous years. Use the Blue Book for this. For instance, for a three-year lease, see how much a similar car sold for in 1987 compared to its worth in 1990. See how much a similar car sold for in 1988 compared to its 1991 worth, etc.

♦ If buying a performance model of a car, are you being hit with a lower residual value? Argue that performance cars usually sell for more than their usual value.

Things to Negotiate

♦ Negotiate the lease end purchase option.(This is the price you would pay to buy the leased vehicle at the end of the lease.) Try to get the same interest rate as the initial lease. Make the purchase optional.

♦ Negotiate any premature buyout option.
♦ Negotiate any involuntary buyout option.
♦ What happens if the car is totalled?
♦ Discuss prepayment options.
♦ How much is gap insurance? If a car is stolen or destroyed, the insurance payment is usually less than the amount of money still owed on the vehicle. Gap insurance covers this "gap."

♦ What about repairs and guarantees? Who does the repairs? Is it the warranty from the factory? Who handles damage due to accidents or acts of nature?

♦ What sort of insurance requirements are demanded?

Things to Clarify

♦ Discuss the condition of the car at lease end. Make sure you are not stuck buying new tires. Ask about any small dings, fabric rips, and equipment that doesn't work (i.e., power options). Get a firm *written* description of what is allowable and what is not.

♦ How many miles are allowed yearly? What sort of penalties are assessed for overages on miles? Are there credits for mileage under the allowance?

♦ Try not to accept a large disposition fee. A disposition fee is a fee to take the vehicle back into the dealership from you at the end of the lease. There is no logic for this cost, it is just a way to get more money from you, the consumer. This fee illustrates how sneaky leasing can be. In buying a new car, all the costs are up front. In leasing, many of the costs show up in the end, thereby making leasing appear cheaper initially.

LEASING CHECKLIST

_____ 1. Interest rate.

_____ 2. Is it an APR or simple interest?

_____ 3. Length of the lease.

_____ 4. Interest rate for purchase of the car at the end of the lease.

_____ 5. Price guarantee of the car at the end of the lease.

_____ 6. Does the interest rate change if I lease or if I buy?

_____ 7. Does the price or financing change if I lease or if I buy?

Remember, negotiate the vehicle price *first*, then discuss leasing, then negotiate such items as interest rate, residual value of the vehicle, etc. Base your lease costs on that amount.

16

Financing

This is where it all comes together. Once you've decided whether to buy or lease, you are ready to enter the last stage of the car buy — financing. (Remember the order of the buy?)

This is the place where you get everything together and see what it is you are going to pay and how you are going to pay it. This is the place where your power is the strongest. This is the place where you will be most aware of your power and the most careful not to blow the deal. The main difference between buying a car and financing it is that you will be dealing with a different specialist with different tricks.

Remember, before you go to the showroom, you have done your homework. This includes having your non-dealer financing approved. You have gone to a bank, credit union, or your favorite uncle and gotten the best loan for your vehicle. Know the dollar amount, the number of months, and the APR.

By now, you have fought really hard and gotten a price approaching Blue Book wholesale for your trade-in. You have also gotten a price close to dealer's cost plus about $300 for that beautiful new car. Now is the time to put it all together, not to let anything slip away, and not to get hit with any additional costs. Remember that there are four segments to a car transaction and while you have just managed two of them (trade-in price and new car price). You still have the financing and the purchasing of special items to go. Before we get into these two points, let's see some of the things that the dealership may legitimately ask you to do or sign to expedite the transactions. Here are some things you may have to sign:

◆ Power of attorney to allow the dealership to pay off your trade-in and/or register your new car for you. Sometimes, you will have to sign two of these forms so that they can repossess your vehicle if necessary.

◆ State law may mandate that you sign off that certain things have been explained to you. Beware that some dealerships try to use this signing off to pressure you into making a purchase.

♦ You may have to authorize the dealership to look at your credit report if you finance through them.

OPTIONS

In addition to signing off on the above items, you will be pressured by the finance person to buy certain extras and options. They certainly will not tell you which of these items are worth your money and which are not. Let's look at the options with your value in mind:

♦ Extended warranty — never pay full price for the extended warranty. It may be worth your while to have this, *if* the price is right and you are worried about repairs. You may be able to get it for up to fifty percent off. Just keep asking and watch the price drop. Dealerships will try for $150 plus per year of coverage. A six-year extended warranty would cost you $900 and $150 per year! Dealerships will accept considerably less, but only if you push for it. Also, this is one item that you do not have to buy now; you can buy it later if you want.

♦ Life insurance — pass on this. This is a car dealership, buy your life insurance from a reputable insurance agent.

♦ Loans or financing — take dealership financing only if: (1) you can get it for less than your financing from an outside source, and (2) you expect to keep the car for the full term. You should get a discount on percentage rates of one half point (percent) in order to compensate for the Rule of 78 financing sold at dealerships.

♦ Anti-theft devices — no recommendations here either way. Only you will know if this is a necessary expense. Before you purchase the one offered by the dealership, see if you can get a markedly reduced price. There are lots of systems on the market if you want one—shop around first if this is an item you would seriously want.

♦ Rustproofing — the experts say this is probably not needed and is way too expensive. Another clever way for the dealership to help you part with your money.

♦ Outside car care package—nice as it makes the car look, this package has a very high markup. See if you can get the price reduced by fifty to sixty-six percent. Better yet, see if you can avoid paying for it and have them leave it on the car you are buying. Remember, at a low enough price, everything is an attractive purchase. (An alternative to their package is to buy the products and apply them yourself.)

♦ Inside car care package — if you really want it, get the price way down. Same as the outside package.

♦ Radios and sound systems — outside sound systems from outside sources are very good and often less expensive. In addition, these sources install and warranty their product. If you know you want a good sound system, investigate before going in to the dealership.

RULE OF 78

Throughout this book, I have referred to the most common financing done by car dealers as Rule of 78 financing. Most people who have never worked in the car business have never heard of Rule of 78. Here is a review of this loan type so that you can be better informed of its details and decide what is the best option for you:

1. All loans are broken into two parts: principal (the amount borrowed) and interest (what it is costing you to borrow the principal).
2. In Rule of 78, the interest over the entire life of the loan is divided by 78. There are 78 equal "pieces" of the interest on your loan.
3. The first monthly payment made on a Rule of 78 loan consists of twelve of these pieces of interest with the remainder of the payment being principal repayment. The second monthly payment made on a Rule of 78 loan consists of eleven of these pieces of interest with the remainder of the payment being principal repayment. And so on until the twelfth monthly payment which consists of one piece of this interest with the rest of the payment being principal repayment.

    12 (parts of interest paid the first month) + 11 (parts paid the second month) + 10 + 9 + 8 + 7 + 6 + 5 + 4 + 3 + 2 + 1 (part of interest paid on the twelfth month) = 78. Hence the Rule of 78.
4. In the first year, all of the interest for the life of the loan has been paid. All future payments are principal only.

Rule of 78 is a financing gimmick set up to extract all of the interest in a loan early in the loan payment period. You pay off all of the interest and very little of the principal. It is true that if you keep your loan until its expiration date and nothing else happens, it doesn't matter if your loan package is Rule of 78 or simple interest. But what happens if you get in an accident and the insurance company pays off on the car? You will have paid off all the interest, and the insurance will cover only a percentage of the remaining principal value of the car. You will be stuck for the difference.

Rule of 78 is great for the dealership. They get their interest paid to them early in the financing contract. But more important, if you decide to refinance later to take advantage of a lowering in interest rates, most of the interest has already been paid off but you will be refinancing a large principal balance. Good for them, not good for you.

THE BUSINESS OF FINANCING

Now that you understand Rule of 78, let's look at what actually happens in the finance room. The first item on the agenda is to confirm that the finance person agrees with the prices you and the salesperson negotiated earlier. This must be done before you begin discussing the details such as length of financing, interest rate, lease vs. buying, etc. Let's look at the items to be discussed with the finance person.

1. Reaffirm the cost of the new car. Make sure he knows what you have agreed to pay for the new vehicle. Make sure you both agree on the items that will be on the vehicle. Don't negotiate. If he balks at the price, show him the figures you have written down and call in the sales manager if necessary. There should be no surprises here.

2. Reaffirm the price given you on your trade-in. Go back to your notes, have him reaffirm that this price is fixed, firm, and solid and that there will not be a sudden change in what you are given for it.

3. Reaffirm the amount of down payment needed. Dealerships love cash; make sure that the amount of down payment doesn't suddenly rise.

4. Recheck the amount of rebates, first time buyer money, etc. This is all free cash to the dealership, but it is your free cash. If there is factory-to-consumer cash, it will be presented to you here. Make sure that the price for the new car does not have this included in it already. It is important to have it made crystal clear that rebate money was not negotiated into the low price you got for the new car. Factory-to-dealer cash, on the other hand, is negotiated in the sales room when getting the best price for your new vehicle. American car manufacturers typically give factory-to-consumer cash, while Japanese car companies provide more factory-to-dealer incentives.

5. Reaffirm the amount of package discounts. Make sure that there is no mistake in this figure. If you have been promised power steering at no charge because you bought the air-conditioning system, make sure the finance person honors the commitment made to you earlier.

6. Ask about items such as alarm systems, extra pinstripes, extended warranty, etc. Make a firm decision of yes or no on each one, then negotiate price. Review the list above on these items. Remember the high markup and try to cut price by at least half or most items are not even worth considering.

7. Ask how much time you have before your option to buy an extended warranty expires. Also ask if there is any other organization that will offer you an extended warranty on the car later.

8. Ask about their best financing package before telling them that you have financing from an outside source. Once you have their information, compare it to the financing you have already obtained. Check for Rule of 78 financing. When you mention your outside financing, ask them to beat your package. Tell him that you would rather the finance money go to the dealership than to the bank. Make sure they express the loan percentage in APR (Annual Percentage Rate), the loan amount in an actual dollar figure, the monthly payments, and the number of months. Check your chart or calculator to make sure that these figures make sense and are correct for the loan amount you are borrowing.

The dealership may offer you financing, but some of the terms of this financing will differ from that offered by your friendly local bank or credit union. Most dealerships offer interest rates that are based on the Rule of 78. Most outside lending institutions use a method with interest on the declining balance of the loan.

FINANCING CHECKLIST

This list is meant to help you gather facts to show you how much your car purchase is really going to cost after everything has been added up. Make guesses for numbers 1-19 as sort of a practice run before going to the dealership so you have a rough idea of what the costs will be. Then fill the whole list during the financing part of the buy. Obviously, you will have items #1 and #2 before going to the showroom.

1. Lender _____
   interest rate _____% (APR) amount of loan _____
   type of loan _____
2. Lender _____
   interest rate _____% (APR) amount of loan _____
   type of loan _____
3. Dealership _____
   interest rate _____% (APR) amount of loan _____
   type of loan _____
4. Cost of new car (from your negotiations) _____
5. Trade-in value (from your negotiations) _____
6. Down payment (including trade-in) _____
7. Amount of dealer rebate _____
8. Amount of package discounts (luxury package, etc.) _____
9. Amounts of other discounts and rebates (first time buyer, promotional discounts, etc.) _____
10. Sales tax _____% x _____ (price) = _____

11. Registration and licensing fees _____
12. Document fee _____
13. Insurance _____
14. Other items (extended warranty, etc.) _____
15. Transportation (freight) _____
16. Dealer's prep (this is usually included at no cost) _____
17. Initial gas and oil (should be included in price) _____
18. Dealer's advertising (I would never pay this one) _____
19. Figure the amount to be financed (4 less 5, 6, 7, 8, and 9 plus 10, 11, 12, 13, 14, 15, and 16) _____
20. Monthly payments for _____ months at _____ APR = _____

LEASING FINANCING CHECKLIST

Remember, negotiate the vehicle price *first*, then discuss leasing. After you decide that you are going to lease you can negotiate such items as interest rate, residual value of the vehicle, etc. Base your lease amount on those figures.

If you are considering leasing, here are some other important questions to ask in financing.

1. What is the interest rate (APR)? _____
2. What is the length of the lease? _____
3. Is the lease figured simple interest? _____
4. What is the interest rate for purchase of the car at the end of the lease? _____
5. What is the price guarantee of the car at the end of the lease? ___
6. Is there any difference between the leasing and buying interest rates? _____
7. Is there any difference between the leasing and buying price or financing? _____
8. Have the dealership spell out the condition the car must be in on return to avoid a penalty. _____
9. What is the maximum mileage per year? Are there penalties for exceeding this? _____
10. How much is the return fee? _____
11. Are there any other fees on return of the car? _____

ITEMS TO DOUBLECHECK

♦ Have you been charged only for items you specifically wanted? (no extras)

- Did you get all factory cash, first time buyer's discount, etc?
- Was there was anything else promised that the dealer conveniently forgot or nibbled away?
- Ask what else they can do for you or give you to make the high cost of the car more palatable. Perhaps they will throw in a cargo net or some sort of an upgrade or a free oil and lube on your first service visit.
- Have the finance person write up the contract and put figures on paper. Make sure each figure is explained.
- Ask the finance person if anything was added to the pricing of the car that you did not specifically request, but that he thought you might need or want.
- Is the car a refugee from the lemon law? In California and other states with a lemon law, consumers are allowed to return a new car to the dealership if the car has an inordinate number of mechanical problems and/or need of repair.
- Is the car a flood car? A flood car is a new car that has been water damaged, rebuilt, and offered for sale as a new car.
- Is the car damaged, was it in an accident and fixed up? Occasionally a brand new car is stolen from a dealership, damaged, recovered, and fixed up. This sort of trauma to a new car should be disclosed to the customer.
- Is there anything about the car that I should know about in order to make an informed decision?
- Have there been any recalls on this type of car? What type?
- What is the length of guarantee on this car?
- Does the dealership provide loaner cars or transportation if the car needs covered repairs?
- Is the car really new? Has it ever been registered before?
- Did you get everything you asked for? Has anything been omitted or held back? (Check your list made during negotiations.)
- Doublecheck all of the numbers used to price your car (in case of inadvertent substitution or error).
- If there are repairs or substitutions promised you, hold back a part of the money until they are completed or else refuse to sign until they are completed.
- Check to make sure that no fees were tacked on after the final figure has been decided upon (such as dealer's prep fee which usually is included in the price of the car).
- Ask for them to throw in some free floor mats when you sign.

17

New Car-Buying Wrap-Up

Now you are armed with just about everything you need to know about how to buy a car, except the actual experience. Using the very practical information provided in the book and tabulated in the lists, you should be set to test yourself in a practice mode against experienced auto dealers. But as the Boy Scouts say, "Be Prepared." Research your car before you buy; price your trade-in before you try to trade it in; shop for financing before you go to a showroom; and calculate what new cars cost the dealers before you negotiate price. Also, see what the auto experts (and your friends and neighbors) think of the car you want to buy, and see if the flaws they see bother you. At the very least use these perceived flaws to negotiate a better deal on the car. Be prepared for all the salesperson's tactics by knowing what they usually use.

Now that you have done your homework, there are just a couple of words of wisdom left.

♦ Don't go looking for cars if you are rushed, tired, sick, or not confident that you will do a good job.
♦ Nothing else works like perseverance; don't get discouraged or give in. Hang tough.
♦ Don't tell any salesperson anything more about you than necessary.
♦ Don't bring anyone with you who can't or won't help you.
♦ When you are near an agreement, try saying no one more time to see what happens.

COMMON QUESTIONS

Potential car buyers seem to be consistently concerned or confused about certain issues. These are some of the common questions I have heard and my responses to them.

Q. Can I drive so good a deal that the dealership or salesperson loses money on me?

A. Barring a major accident, they won't sell you the car if it doesn't make them some money or if the deal isn't beneficial for the dealership.

Q. Does the type of dealership make a difference in how good a deal I can get?

A. It makes some difference. Larger dealerships may be able to offer lower prices under certain circumstances. It may be more difficult for the smallest dealers to offer large discounts. In general, however, the final price is determined by the economy more than by any other factor, including size.

Q. Do all those great sale blitzes and sale spectaculars really mean a cheaper price or a better deal?

A. Again, the economy is the determining factor in the deal, the price on your trade-in, the new car price, the rebates, etc. Holding the sale with bales of hay and a salesperson wearing a cowboy hat is just show biz. When you see a sale, see what is new; is there a higher rebate? Are they dumping year old/new cars? If you can't see what is new, the sale is just a way of getting attention. Dealers won't sell a car at a loss, so a sale won't get you a better than good negotiation unless something extra is thrown in. Treat a sale like a call for new business, not a special price break unless there is something new. Factory-to-consumer cash is a real discount, factory-to-dealer cash may not be.

Q. What is the best buy, a domestic or a foreign car?

A. Quality used to be the overriding feature that provided an advantage for the European and Japanese cars. I don't believe this is true now. The Japanese, but not the Europeans, have a slight advantage in quality, but it is so small that other factors have a strong influence. With quality essentially equal and that small difference compensated for by the excellent warranties on domestic cars, both are acceptable. I firmly believe that you can really do well on American car dealers with respect to price. It always seems more difficult to get the Japanese car dealers to drop their prices. Therefore, I recommend that you buy American but get a great deal.

My final bit of advice on buying a new car is to buy American and keep the extra in your pocket. Not only is this patriotic, it is frugal and makes sense *if* the car is right for you. Don't rule out an American car based on past history. Consider what they are like now.

Now that you have all the tools to do a great job, if you want that great *new* car just go out and buy it. If you want to look at getting a great used car, or if you want to sell your used car yourself, read the following chapters and see how it,s done. It is easy, exhilarating, and very profitable. Even if you don't think you want a used car, I strongly suggest that you consider a low mileage used car for the right price and from the right sources. Read the next section before you rule out buying a used car.

Section II
Buying and Selling Used Cars

18

New Cars vs. Used Cars

Almost everybody, if given unlimited money, would buy an expensive new car with all the extras. We would all also like to live in a mansion, eat at the best restaurants, buy the best of everything, and not worry about spending at all. However, we are not able to do all that we want. If we go for the new car with all the trimmings, we may have to forgo eating and air conditioning.

Since we know that new cars are expensive, let's look analytically at the reasons for choosing to buy one. Let's examine these reasons closely to see if they are really valid reasons.

REASONS FOR GETTING A NEW CAR

REASON 1: I don't want to buy anybody else's trouble.
RESPONSE: Buying a used car does not necessarily mean buying another person's troubles any more than buying a new car is always a trouble-free experience. That reason is usually an excuse for being afraid to look for a great used car.
REASON 2: I have enough money; cost isn't an issue and I want a brand new car.
RESPONSE: Can't argue with this one — buy that new car and enjoy it. The average person has to balance her spending. I personally prefer to spend less on cars and more on other items.
REASON 3: When I buy a new car the dealer takes care of everything. I don't have to do a lot of extra legwork.
RESPONSE: True, but you pay an awful lot for that saved legwork.
REASON 4: I have such bad credit that if I have to buy a car I need a dealer to take care of all the financial details and get me some credit.
RESPONSE: Some dealerships *will* sell you a car if your credit is bad, but they protect themselves and take you on the terms, interest rate, etc. If your credit is bad, why would you choose to pay more than necessary for a product and risk owing even more money?

REASON 5: I need long-term warranties to take care of any possible problems and you can only get them with a new car.

RESPONSE: Warranties are also available at "after market warranty" places. Warranties are great for giving you peace of mind, but you do not need to pay dealer prices for that peace of mind. Take your newly purchased used car to the dealership and see if there is an extended warranty that can be reactivated. If not, see if they will sell you one at a reasonable price.

REASON 6: It is very important to me that I get the exact color, style, options that I want. It is possible to get exactly what I want only in a new car.

RESPONSE: If you can afford it, go for it. If money is a consideration and you feel you can compromise on some of these demands, consider a great used car. You might be pleasantly surprised.

REASON 7: I want the bragging rights that come with a new car.

RESPONSE: Bragging rights do come with a new car, and they are powerful bragging rights indeed. However, you can counter that brag with the information that your car cost sixty-five percent of the cost of the same car new. The really impressive bragging happens when you compare your monthly payments to that new car owner and indicate that you expect to spend Christmas in Hawaii with his car dealer.

REASON 8: New cars are better than used cars and I deserve the best.

RESPONSE: New cars are better mechanically than old cars, but for the price not all new cars are better than all used cars. For example, which is better: a brand new $17,000 Chevy Lumina with all the bells and whistles and no miles or a one year-old Cadillac Sedan DeVille with 15,000 miles obtained at auction for $17,000?

REASONS FOR GETTING A USED CAR

1. The main reason for getting a used car is money. Used cars are cheap compared to new cars and you do get more for your money.

2. A car loses as much as fifty percent of its value at the end of its first year. Look through any of the Edmund's new car price guides. You will quickly see that at the end of the first year, some cars drop in value by more than half! It takes only four more years (on average) to drop another twenty-five percent so that at the end of five years, many cars are down to twenty-five percent of their original price.

If money is a factor, the best way to buy a car is to forgo the new car smell and get a car at half-price.

I feel that the best car bargains are used cars. The best bargains in used cars are year-old vehicles with low mileage. These cars have already lost a large percent of their original value, but are still practically new.

Consider this: if you buy a $25,000 shiny leather-seated car, drive it off the lot and return with it in two months to trade it in, even if it only has 5,000 miles on it, the trade-in value will be $17,000.

This is a substantial decrease in value. One of the main reasons is that a lot of the items you buy with a new car have absolutely no resale value. These include:

♦ Transportation. This fee varies from $200 to over $500. There is no way they will give you credit for this on a trade-in.

♦ Title, taxes, and registration.

♦ Document, insurance, or title fees. There may be a a whole host of little fees that your dealership tacks on (or must tack on by law). These also have no resale value.

♦ Leasing fees or penalties for early return of the vehicle.

♦ Dealer's advertising fee. I warned you earlier not to pay this one, but some car dealers break out an extra charge for this, even though it would seem to be part of their normal operating expenses.

♦ Special packages. Remember that special exterior finish and pinstripe combination for which you paid $350? The next buyer won't pay for your artistic taste and may even consider unusual exterior markings a deduction. There is no way they will give you any credit for those items.

♦ Special interior treatments. Remember those marvelous floor mats and the rest of that stuff for which you paid an additional $500 when you found out that it was already included on the car you wanted to buy? Well, you won't get any credit for that either.

♦ AMU or ADMU. You wanted a hot car and paid extra for it. They won't pay extra to take it back.

♦ Dealer's profit over cost.

♦ Dealer's prep. Some dealerships will try to charge you for this as an extra even though it is and should be included in the cost of the car.

This list doesn't even include wear and tear and normal depreciation on the vehicle itself. This just points out items for which you paid and will never recoup. These are costs you will never recover, costs that contribute to the car's phenomenal depreciation its first year.

Can you stand the uncertainty of buying a car that is not quite new if you can save a lot of money in the process? I hope so. A good used car is a great financial savings and should be considered for that reason alone. Most of the advantages of a new car can also be found in a *nearly* new car.

19

Options for Buying a Used Car

Once you've decided to purchase a used car, there are essentially four ways to do it. (There is also a fifth way that is so rare that it should be considered a gift rather than a legitimate buy.) Let's look at these in detail and see which suits you best as a way of getting a used vehicle that is inexpensive, safe, and reliable.

First, let's look at the used car market and its relationship to the new car market. For the past several years, the new car market has been in a slump. The number of new cars sold has been much lower than expected, and the average age of the U.S. car fleet has risen each year. Every year Detroit comes out with new models and expects a great new design to magically spur car sales and save their corporate buns. The age of the U.S. car population will continue to increase for a while because the cars are better made (thanks to the Japanese for making the U.S. auto makers produce better cars). Cars no longer rust as easily or wear out as easily, and new vehicles keep increasing in cost. With fewer new cars being sold, there are fewer good trade-ins available. So the supply of good used cars gets lower but the demand for affordable transportation keeps rising.

Why does the price of new cars keep rising? They are more expensive because they have expensive safety equipment. They are more expensive because there are engineering costs brought on by the mileage requirements of the government. They are more expensive because to lower the weight of a car you must use more expensive lightweight materials. Pollution and emission controls don't help to lower the price of vehicles either. Whatever the reasons, they are still more expensive. So it becomes more difficult to buy a $25,000 Buick. But people still have to get to work, people still want their kid to have a car for college, families still need a second car. So if you can't afford that new car you are forced to get a good used car. People will get that good used car even if they have to pay a couple of bucks more for it. It is a lot easier to afford a good used $6,000 Buick than a beautiful brand new $25,000 one.

"When my job is secure and when my wife gets back to work and when my oldest son is finished with college, *then* I will get that beautiful new Buick that I really want," you may say. "But until then, I will make do with a good used car, even if I have to pay a lot more for it than it is really worth."

Now, every time a new car is not bought, the price of new cars drops a little. Every time a used car is bought by someone who would really rather have a new car, the price of all used cars rises slightly because there is one fewer of them. What we are seeing is the resultant drop of the possible profit margins on new cars and the rising price of used cars. This trend cannot continue indefinitely. It can only go on so far before it becomes worthwhile for more people to start to buy new cars again.

When used car prices are very high and new cars are practically being given away, it becomes more important than ever to buy that used car well. There are only four ways to do this (not including "The Gift Way," but I am including it because it only occurs in your wildest dreams).

THE GIFT

Uncle Albert dies at the age of seventy-eight, and Aunt Edith doesn't drive. You (little Al) were Uncle Al's favorite grandnephew and rather than selling his car to a stranger whose very presence would defile the memory of her wonderful saintly husband of fifty-three years, Aunt Edith gives you the $8000 Buick for only $500 because you are still in school and because the money isn't really that important to her. Since it was only driven to church and back, it has only 30,000 miles. This does not happen very often. Now you see why I treat this as a special case.

FROM A NEW CAR DEALERSHIP

Advantages

1. Selection. There is usually a good selection of nearly new used cars of the type the dealership sells.
2. Accountability. This is a licensed dealer. You may receive a guarantee and you know they will be there tomorrow. If they defraud you, you can go for a legal remedy or to the state boards and get relief. This is your most reputable option.
3. Financing. Longer term financing is probably available.

4. Condition. This is your best chance for the used cars to be in tip-top shape. They may not be, but this is your best chance.
5. Good title. The car should have good title. (If not, you have legal recourse.)

Disadvantages

1. Sales staff. The sales force is tough, hard, and well-trained. (You can deal with them by following the guidelines listed in the first part of this book.)
2. High financing. The financing is higher than you would pay at a bank. (You can beat this by obtaining outside financing as outlined earlier.)
3. Limited choices. These places usually don't have older used cars. There are probably not more than 150 vehicles in their lot.
4. Cost. You will pay top dollar here.

FROM A NON-DEALERSHIP LOT

Non-dealership lots are run by licensed dealers, usually sole proprietors or a limited number of partners. These things spring open, run for a couple of years and go out of business without notice. These lots sometimes specialize, but usually they carry whatever the owner can get from a wholesaler or an auction or from people who come in trying to sell their old car and buy another old car. These small lots have a variety of service people who come to the lot; detail people, battery fixers, mechanics, parts deliverers, etc. The cars here may or may not be of the best quality. The place thrives on credit sales where the buyer of the vehicle puts out a high down payment, usually about equal to the owner's interest in the car and pays off the loan weekly in less than a year. The lot owner sells cars quickly and repossesses them nearly as quickly.

Advantages

1. Credit. Some credit is available, but it is usually short-term.
2. The dealer is licensed and therefore accountable.
3. The cars probably have good title.

Disadvantages

1. The sales force is tough and hard.
2. The financing is higher than you would pay at a bank.
3. If you miss a few payments the car will be repossessed.
4. These lots usually have older used cars.
5. There are probably not more than fifty vehicles in their lot.

6. Prices are high. You will pay top dollar here. Their average profit margin per car is very high.
7. Here today, gone tomorrow.
8. The vehicles may or may not be in great shape.

PRIVATE PARTY SALES

This is everybody's secret escape from having to deal with a hard, tough dealer. They know they will find a nice low mileage car put up for sale by a refined old gentleman in a smoking jacket who will serve them lemonade while he cheerfully says, "I really don't know what my car is worth, but if you suggest a reasonable figure I am sure I would agree to it." Of course it is a one owner car, has been garaged all its life, has all the service records, and has had its oil changed religiously every 1500 miles. The car is also mechanically perfect and is offered by the seller with a three-year unconditional warranty.

Unfortunately, buying through a private party doesn't usually work that way. From my experience in California, between one third and one half of the cars sold through the paper are sold by dealers. These dealers buy cars from private parties or auctions, may fix them up, and then resell them. These dealers disguise their identities and initially pose as private parties. Some individuals also make a living by buying low from one person and selling high to another. These people are not the original and only owner of the car for sale. They may well have owned it for only a few days before reselling it at a profit.

Advantages

If everything goes right, this method of private party buying/selling is the best. If it doesn't, it is the worst.

The advantages of a private party buy are:

1. You may get an actual record of repair and maintenance.
2. Most people don't know how to sell, so the price may be right.
3. It may be your easiest buy. The transaction may be friendly, comfortable, and convenient.

Disadvantages

1. There is a possibility of a bad title. Many of these vehicles are of dubious title. Who really knows where the owner got the car, or who the seller really is? The seller may have just bought the car from another party, and gotten the other party to sign over the title. When you give him cash for the car, he will give you the signed title in exchange for cash. When the car is registered this intermediate

seller doesn't appear anywhere on the ownership chain. Trying to get back at him legally if you need to is almost impossible. This is called jumping title. Pay no attention to any promises or guarantees, you will have no way of holding him accountable.

2. No guarantees. You are not dealing with a licensed dealer.
4. No financing.
5. Inconsistency. You can find all sorts of vehicles through the paper and you cannot always trust the descriptions.
6. You will have to ride all over town to see a small number of vehicles.
7. Price will be highly variable. Most owners are not knowledgeable about the worth of their vehicle.
8. The seller may really be a dealer disguised as a private party.
9. You have no recourse if the vehicle turns out to be bad or immediately breaks down.

After comparing the advantages to the disadvantages this doesn't look as safe and easy as you thought, does it? So now you say to yourself, "How can I get a used car through a licensed dealer so that I have some recourse and a guarantee against a bad title, and still do so with a minimum of aggravation for a reasonable price?"

Believe it or not, there is a way. This is my favorite way to buy a car. As a matter of fact I liked it so much I decided to go into that business as soon as I found it existed.

AUCTION BUYING THROUGH A DEALER

In Chapter 1 I told you how I got into the auto business with my first buy of a Dodge Lancer. Learning how to buy the Lancer really taught me how to buy a new car. Let me tell you how I learned to buy used cars.

After I landed in California and bought my Lancer, which my wife loved, I changed jobs within my company and picked up a company car. Great inventions these company cars; the Boss paid for my gas, oil, repairs, tires, washes, etc., through his budget. When the car, a Ford LTD, reached either three years or 50,000 miles it was scheduled to be turned in for a brand new car.

When this time came, I was in need of another car at home. I thought that this company car would be a natural if I could get it cheaply. So the first thing I did was to put in for new tires, a tune-up, new brakes, etc. I got the car fixed up nicely. It was absolutely immaculate. Then I went into see my boss and asked him if I could buy my company car when they replaced it and, if so, for how much. He got back to me a few days later with a figure that made me wince. He quoted me a figure close to $5000. I gratefully declined to purchase it, but asked him where the car was going. He said it would be returned to our rental agency and from there it would be sold at auction. I called the rental agency and they indicated it would be sold at a dealers only auction. I had them give me the selling date.

It occurred to me that maybe I would get a dealer to buy my company car for me for a small fee. But I had no idea how to find that dealer. At a loss as to what to do, I went back to the dealership that had sold me my Lancer, half-expecting to be thrown out, or at the least, ignored. What I found was that in the year or so since I bought that car, virtually the whole sales force had turned over (not so unusual an occurrence) and only one person, the sales manager, was left. He was also leaving the dealership and it was his last day. He greeted me warmly. When I told him my idea, he promptly gave me the name of a dealer friend who could buy my company car at auction for a fair fee.

Two weeks later I was allowed into the dealers only auction where I watched him buy my company car for $2500, below the maximum bid I had budgeted. The person not only bought me my car but also did all the paperwork, registered the car, and collected the taxes.

The following day I drove my old company car, now my own personal car, to work and left it in my boss's parking spot. Later in the day, I filled him in with the details of the transaction, including the fact that I had had it completely fixed up before I had turned it in. He laughed and said that I had really caught on. He also asked me if I would I do the same for him in the future if he wanted to buy back his company car.

That experience convinced me that the best way to buy a used vehicle, bar none, is to buy it at a dealers only auction through a licensed dealer.

Let's look at this system and see why auction buying of cars through a dealer really works.

Advantages

1. You are buying through a licensed dealer. This is important because it gives you some legal recourse in case something goes wrong. You can always find a dealer. If he moves, the DMV (Department of Motor Vehicles) can find him. He is usually bonded, and the threat of action against his license is strong enough to force him to back down if he is guilty of gross mischief. I know it is tough to think of car dealers as being reputable, but compared to the other possibilities, they are probably okay. My opinion is that all other things being equal, it is better to deal with a licensed and bonded person than just another pretty face. Legal recourse is one advantage that private party sales don't have.

2. Titles are guaranteed at dealers auctions. This may not seem like much until you find out you have bought a car with a salvage title from a Mr. No Name on a street corner. Dealers auctions have car titles that are guaranteed. Therefore, if you buy a car through a dealer at auction , you know you are getting a car that is not stolen and that has some traceability. This is another advantage that private party sales don't have.

3. Reduced chances of fraud. In the buying and selling of property of any kind, especially expensive property, fraud is always a possibility. House sales, which are more highly regulated than auto sales and whose transfer takes more time and is more painstakingly controlled, have their own set of problems. People even spend hundreds of dollars to get a company to guarantee title to a piece of property. No such option exists in the sales of used cars. Private party sales are inherently subject to this type of problem, especially misrepresentation of the physical condition of the vehicle.

    Dealers only auction sales of cars have some built-in safeguards, which revolve around disclosure of mileage, mileage deficiencies, frame damage, fees owing, and other such details.

    The system is not perfect, and fraud undoubtedly occurs. Some of the most commonly attempted deceptions involve rolling back the mileage showing on the odometers of high mileage vehicles and disguising engine or transmission problems. Auction rules requiring disclosure of items like frame damage, mileage, discrepancies of title, DMV fees, etc., are a strong factor in getting what you think you are getting. Most auctions also have some form of a drive train guarantee on certain makes and models.

4. Low prices. This is where auction buying of vehicles really shines. There are two different types of automobile auctions: public auctions and dealers only auctions. Auctions that are open to the public are usually advertised on the back pages of the classified section of the newspapers. These auctions are outlets for the sale of city police vehicles, local government vehicles, etc. Sometimes these are disguised as drug seizure auctions. In an auction of seventy-three cars advertised in this way, you might find two that are from two drug seizures and the newest of these might be a 1985 Chevy Camaro. But the public is caught up in the thought of buying a brand new Porsche for $100. People will go to these auctions and end up paying over retail for vehicles they really don't like because they get caught up in the spirit of the auction.

    The better auctions to buy from are the dealers only auctions.

These are open only to licensed dealers who are registered with one or more of them. These are truly competitive auctions with vehicles supplied from repos, banks, and dealer consignment. The buyers are true dealers who are buying seriously for retail resale from their lots. Retail customers are not allowed into these auctions, so you never see a bidding frenzy fueled by people who are used to buying at retail or higher prices.

Dealers will stop bidding long before a car reaches retail price. After all, how will they then sell those price-inflated vehicles? If they buy a car at auction and the price is too high, how can they cover all the costs in a transaction, including the sales costs, and still make a profit? Dealers aren't even happy about buying a car for Blue Book wholesale; they prefer to get a vehicle for hundreds of dollars below that price. If the price of a car at a dealers only auction goes too high, the dealers just stop bidding and walk away.

This doesn't mean that everything sold in an auction is cheap. There are always special cases where cars go for ridiculous prices. For example, during Operation Desert Storm, the Iraqi army took Kuwait's entire taxi fleet. After the war, Kuwait had to replace all of these vehicles. The southern California auctions saw a huge price rise in cars that could function as taxis. Two- and three-year-old Ford Crown Victorias, Chevy Caprices, and Mercury Grand Marquis were selling at near *retail* at these dealers only auctions. This is almost unheard of and lasted only until the need for those cars in Kuwait was satisfied.

5. Large selection. Typical used car lots vary from the very small lots with only fifteen to twenty cars to the very large lots with several hundred cars. Typical dealers only auctions typically range from 500 to close to 3000 cars. These auctions are held weekly, giving the dealer quite a variety to choose from. You can find virtually anything you want in one of these dealers only auctions.

The sheer volume seems overwhelming and you may wonder where they all come from. The number of cars for sale in just one auction dwarfs those listed for sale in the major southern California newspapers. The advantage for all of those people putting a car up for sale at a dealers only auction is that the car will sell for immediate cash. These cars come from a number of sources.

♦ Repossessed cars or "repos"; cars repossessed from people who have missed payments. Once these cars are repossessed, they belong to the institution that financed them. Typical owners of repos are banks, GMAC finance, etc. The quickest way for these owners to recoup some of their costs is to dispose of the cars at auction.

♦ Leased cars; thirty-five percent of the cars leaving new car lots in California are leased. When these cars come to the end of their leases, they can either be bought by the leasing party or returned to the leasing agency. Most of those returned eventually end up at auction.

♦ Factory demos, executive cars, etc.; most major manufacturers have "leftover" cars that are no longer new. These often are sold at auction.

♦ Theft recoveries and damaged vehicles; insurance companies retrieve these vehicles and sell them at auction. These cars may have flawed titles. For example, recovered vehicles may have salvage titles rather than regular titles.

♦ Dealer overflow; dealers will sometimes accept a vehicle as a trade-in that doesn't fit on their lot. For example, a Cadillac dealership may take a Chevrolet on a trade-in, and it may be company policy not to sell any used vehicle other than a Cadillac. Vehicles like this are sent to the dealers only auctions consignment.

In addition, if a car has been a particularly slow seller for a dealership, they may try to sell it at auction. It is possible that it will sell better in another neighborhood with a different clientele.

Disadvantages

All good things have downsides. Let's look at a few of them:

1. Auction buys are cash buys. In order to buy a car at a dealers only auction, you must be prepared to pay cash. If you arrange your financing beforehand so you can give cash to the dealer who is going to buy you a car at auction, you can pay for the car in cash and pay your bank back later. If you need somebody to hold your hand through the financing, a dealer might do it, but he sure will get paid more for it. That is the beauty *and* the problem with buying a car at auction; you have to have the money at the time of the purchase.

2. Lack of adequate inspection. An auction buy does not lend itself easily to a full test drive of the vehicle or a full mechanical inspection. It will be nearly impossible for you to know everything about the car you are interested in as you would if you were buying it on the street or from a dealer's lot. You may not be able to tell if the brakes need work or check the compression or transmission. You can check most things, and you certainly can spot major problems, but not everything. You may get stuck with a bad car, but every method of car buying has the same potential. There is no way to guarantee a perfect trouble free used car. Partially because of this uncertainty, the cars go lower in price at auction in other settings.

3. If you get the highest bid, it's yours. The rules that allow retail customers to return a sale or change their mind do not apply to auction

buys. Once you have bought it, you cannot decide to buy a different car instead. You will have to figure out a way to sell it; you cannot return it.

Of the ways of buying a used car, dealers only auctions offer the best balance for getting a good deal at a great price. If you decide to try to buy a car in this way, you need a good dealer you can trust to inspect your cars well and to represent you well at the auction. You also want one who is honest and has a reasonable commission structure.

These car dealers do exist and word-of-mouth is usually the best recommendation. If someone you trust recommends a dealer to you, you have more information than you would if you were to walk into a dealership cold. People looking to tap into this market were those I wanted to service when I got my dealer's license. I believe that auction buying is the best option both for myself and for the people who come to me.

This is the way this system works for me (and thus for my customers.)

◆ I will get a call, usually a person recommended by one of my former customers or other contacts. We chat for a while and discuss items like type of car preferred, costs, financing, etc.

◆ I make an appointment and meet the individual at the auction I think will be most likely to fit his needs.

◆ We inspect hundreds of vehicles and pick out the ones that most interest him. We settle my commission, and discuss prices for the vehicle. I help the individual clarify what it is he really wants and talk to him about possible bargains. If the individual is after reliability and price, we talk about stick shift American cars as the best current bargain.

◆ I get a good faith down payment, usually 20% of the vehicle's expected price.

◆ I buy the car(s) we have agreed upon at the next auction if I can do so within the agreed price range.

◆ I buy the car out of the auction with additional funds the customer provides.

◆ If necessary, I have the car smogged, spruced up, and repaired.

◆ The paperwork is done and the car is transferred to the buyer. My fee and the costs for taxes, licensing, smogging, repairs, etc., are taken out of the down payment. Any funds owed to me are paid to me. Any funds owed to the customer are now returned to him.

Now that you know my preference, let me outline the best way to get good results buying a used car in a more conventional way.

20

Answering a Newspaper Ad for a Used Car

After deciding to buy a used car, most people turn to the newspapers or automobile trader magazines first. The key here is to find out if the vehicle is being sold through a private party or a commercial car lot that is using classified advertising. A commercial lot advertising in this way is a different case than an individual selling his or her prized vehicle. The best deals are usually found through private party sales. The strategy is different if you are dealing with a professional.

If you find out that you are dealing with a professional, make sure that you read the first part of this book carefully. All of the information about dealing with a new car salesperson works with a used car salesperson as well.

Many people who are selling an auto have done some research and know about what their car is worth. Individuals selling a car try to get somewhere between low and high Blue Book (wholesale and retail) depending on their individual greed, need, and/or the condition of the car. Dealerships usually deal with a better class of car and there is usually the possibility of some sort of guarantee. They try to sell *above* retail and usually get down to retail only after prolonged negotiation.

TELEPHONE CONTACT

When you answer an ad — even if the ad specifies that the car is being sold by a private party, the first question to ask is, "Are you a dealer or a private party?" There is a lot of deception practiced by dealers in this regard.

QUERY CHECKLIST

Once you have established whether or not you are talking to a dealer, you can go on to the business of inquiring about the car. To save yourself a lot of work and to preserve some sense of control over the negotiation, ask the other party to describe his car first. Then ask for specific details. Here is a checklist to help you out.

Used Car Phone Query Checklist

Car type _____

Year _____

Mileage _____

    Is the mileage real? _____

Engine size _____

Number of doors _____

Type of transmission — stick or automatic _____

Special model or style _____

Color _____

Interior condition _____

Exterior condition _____

Asking price _____

    Is this price negotiable? _____

Power steering _____

Power brakes _____

Cruise control _____

Tilt steering _____

Power seat _____

Leather seats _____

Safety equipment _____

    air bags _____

    antilock brakes _____

Sound system _____

    regular am/fm _____

    cassette deck _____

    compact disk _____

    other premium sound items _____

Special light group _____

Special luxury group _____

Special wheels _____

Special tires _____

Floor pads _____

Are the service records available? _____

Is the car title on hand?   _____

Is there any lien holder on the vehicle?   _____

Has the car ever been in an accident?   _____

Other questions or comments   _____

The best technique is to keep the interview focused on your questions, so that you do not get bamboozled with lots of statements about how nice the car is. Your job is to find out as much as you can without having to actually go see every car you call about. Their job is to make their car sound fantastic. Let your fingers do the walking by filling out the above chart rather than spend your day driving all over town. Remember their goal is to get you to go see their car. Yours is to get the most information in the most time-efficient manner, which means not wasting your time and gas going to see unsuitable cars. In small towns, this may not be a major problem, but in larger suburban areas it can be a tremendous waste of time and energy.

Additional Questions

In addition to the telephone query checklist, there are several strategic negotiating questions that will help you determine more about the car.

1. Why are you selling the car? (You may or may not get a real answer, but you won't get anything if you don't ask.)
2. Are you the original owner? (Do not automatically accept yes as the truth.)
3. What is wrong with the car? (Never ask what the condition the car is in. Everybody always says, "Excellent.")
4. If this is a recreational vehicle, has it ever been offroaded or rolled?
5. Is the price negotiable? (Almost everyone will say yes — especially to someone they perceive as a serious buyer.)
6. What is the bottom-line price?
7. Where exactly are you located? (See if there is any way that the seller will give concessions to entice you to go see the car. Also, ask if the seller will bring the car to you. The answer is almost always no, but if it is yes, the seller may be desperate.)
8. How is the body condition?
   Is there any rust?
   Has the car been in any accidents?
9. How new are the tires?
   Do you still have the receipts and warranty?
10. Will you guarantee the car?

11. How long has the car been on the market? (The longer it has been for sale, the more likely the price is negotiable.)

12. Has the car had any recent repairs?
    Do you still have the service records?

13. (Ask again) What price do you need for the car?
    Would you consider $_____ below that price?

14. Do you own the car outright or is there still money owed on it? (This is a key question. If there is money owed on the car, it may be difficult to get the lien removed.)

15. Are you in a hurry to sell the car? (If he/she has to sell the car fast, he/she may accept less money.)

16. Have you had a mechanic look at your car since you put it on the market?
    Is it a problem if I have my mechanic look it over? (See if the seller will take the car to your mechanic. See if the seller will pay for the inspection if you do end up buying the car.)

17. How good is the paint?

18. What is the Blue Book retail and wholesale for the car? (Even if you know — ask.)

19. Will you pay for the smogging or smog inspection and any work necessary to pass the testing if the car fails the inspection?

20. When was the last tuneup?
    If it has been a while, ask: Will you pay for a tuneup?
    If not, will you pay half the cost of a tuneup?

21. Is the car registered in your state? (Out of state registrations may be difficult to transfer and out of state cars may not pass an incoming state inspection — mechanical or smog.)

22. Ask anything else that interests you. Remember, you don't know what you will find out or what they may give away.

23. Try to get the seller to talk price concessions over the phone. If he does, he is desperate or naive. Both are desirable characteristics in a seller.

WHEN YOU SEE THE CAR

When you actually see the car, be reserved but not overly negative. A neutral stance is always the best negotiating stance. If you decide that you are interested in the car, you have neither committed yourself by your enthusiasm nor put off the seller by your negativity.

If you do want to look more closely at a car you have explored over the phone, take it for a test drive and have a mechanic look at it. Remember that you asked the seller to pay for this inspection if you buy the car. If the test drive and the inspection are both satisfactory, decide if you want to buy the car. Here are some tips to help you in the negotiating process.

Negotiating Tips

♦ If the seller is anxious to get rid of the car, make a very low initial offer and stick with it. He may take a low offer from a serious buyer if the car has been on the market for a long time.

♦ Always bring along the money to pay for the car. If you really like it, cash will allow you to demand and get major reductions in the vehicle's price. Cash up front is a rare sight to those living on weekly or monthly salary checks. + As suggested earlier, if you live a long distance from the other party, have him come to you. He will command a much lower price in your back yard if he feels he may have to go all the way home empty-handed.

I know that it is difficult to haggle or to try to get a better price (especially if the seller seems really nice, or reminds you of your Aunt Mary). But look at it from a practical viewpoint: would you rather avoid all the hassles and aggravation and pay this private party his/her fair price and drive off in a glow of friendship and good fellowship and have to work three extra weeks at a job you don't really like to make up the $1500 you gave away by not negotiating hard? Or would you rather prepare well, go in smoothly and efficiently, get that car at your price, come out a winner, have a great feeling of accomplishment, develop a life skill that will earn you money for years to come and incidentally take a vacation with the money you saved?

Here are some questions to ask and some items to look our for. Many of these questions were explored in your initial telephone query, but you cannot really get the answers until you are looking at the car and talking face to face with the seller. You must find out the following information. If you do not, you may be unpleasantly surprised when you try to register the car you just paid for.

1. Has the car ever been in an accident?
2. Does the car need major or minor work body or mechanical work?
3. Was the car ever physically or mechanically abused?
4. Is there any guarantee at all?
5. What is the car really worth? (Compare records, appearance, etc., with your research, as there is no published MSRP.)
6. What does your mechanic say about the vehicle?
7. Does the seller have legal title?
8. Does the seller owe money on the car?

21

Evaluating a Used Car

Everyone's worst nightmare about buying a used car is of getting stuck with a real lemon. In the section on new cars, we discussed the criteria for evaluating a new car. You can safely assume that if a new car seems suitable, the manufacturer will back it up. This is not the case with most used cars. With used cars, you have to find out much more mechanical and technical information before you can feel confident in your purchase.

People tell me all the time that they are reluctant to buy a used car from an auction, a private party, *or* a dealership because they are not automobile mechanics and cannot adequately evaluate a used car. In this chapter, I will show you how to make a reasonable evaluation of a car. I hope that this will give you some measure of confidence.

I am not a mechanic. I cannot rip apart a car and put it back together. I may change my own oil, but that's it. I am not bragging about this, and I wish that I knew more about fixing and evaluating cars, but I don't at this point. I will probably never know enough to repair my own engines, and, quite frankly, I don't really ever want to have to fix my own transmissions. But that doesn't mean I don't know auto mechanics, use auto mechanics, or ask the advice of people who are mechanically skilled.

BASICS

Mechanics Inspection

You don't have to be a mechanic; you just have to use a mechanic. If at all possible, have the car evaluated by a competent mechanic. Have him check the compression, suspension, tires, percentage of the brakes remaining, etc., open up the transmission, and if possible, do an electrical check on the vehicle. Remember to try and convince the seller to pay for the mechanic's inspection *if* you buy the car. This might be enough incentive to convince him to agree. As to what is a fair price to pay for a mechanic? Sorry folks, I can't give you an answer; this is one thing you are going to have to negotiate all by yourself.

If you get the car cheaply enough, you can afford to take more risks in the purchase. In other words, most repairs are acceptable if the buying price is good enough.

Legalities

It would be nice to assume that every car is being sold by its real owner, but this is not always the case. Check for the following:

♦ Is there a lien on the vehicle? Is it signed off? You may want to check with the lienholder to make sure it is really signed off.

♦ Does the VIN (Vehicle Identification Number) on the title match the VIN on the car? Does the description also match?

♦ Does the car have a restricted title such as a salvage title?

♦ Check with your local police department or the State Department of Motor Vehicles to make sure the car is not stolen or does not have title problems. Make sure that the *registered* owner is the one selling the car.

♦ Get the name, address, phone number, and place of business (etc.) of the seller so you can track him down if you need to. If you know where he lives, and who he really is, you have some way to rectify problems.

ASSESSING THE CAR

The items that were covered in the first part of this book are mentioned here as well. I suggest you review the chapter on the test drive before going to look at a used car.

Suitability

Is the car suitable? Do you like the car? A vehicle you hate but buy because you can't resist the price is not a good deal.

Exterior

When inspecting the outside of a vehicle, I make a few circles around the car and answer these questions:

1. Is there any broken or pitted glass?
2. Is the paint in good condition?
3. Are there any indications of a repaint job? Good clues include: orange peel texture, over-spray painting on chrome, rubber, door jambs, or under the hood, and mismatched paints. Signs of a repaint job are usually signs of an accident.

4. Is there any major structural damage? Look for wavy body panels or mismatched colors of paint. Use a magnet (one of those soft refrigerator ones) and check to make sure that all body parts are metal. Often accidents are repaired used a non-metal called Bondo® as fill material. The magnet will reveal its presence. Look in the trunk and under the pads in the back for any indications of corrected rear end damage.

5. Is there any minor structural damage? Look for loose trim, bent side mirrors, missing antennas, missing gas caps, broken door handles, loose bumpers, etc.

6. Is there damage to the paint? Look for door dings, paint scratches, and fading or peeling paint.

7. Are the headlights and tail lights intact? Do they work properly? What about the signals?

8. Are the floor mats with the vehicle?

9. Ask if the car has been garaged during its lifetime. See if the answer meshes with the condition of the car.

10. If the car is a four-wheel drive, ask if it has been offroaded. Look for evidence that it has been offroaded. Dings, especially roof damage, are strong evidence of offroading.

11. How are the tires? Look for good tread and even wear. If they are worn unevenly, they may need to be aligned or replaced. Put your hands on the tires; if the tread is cupped, you may have a strut or shock problem.

    Also note if the tire rims are upscale or base rims. If the car has base rims, ask if you can have the upscale rims if he has any.

Anybody with a good eye can check the exterior and thus get a good indication of the care and maintenance of the car. It should be relatively easy to spot evidence of prior neglect or an accident.

Interior

The goal of inspecting the interior is two-fold. You want to see if the vehicle has been abused and you also want to see if you feel comfortable inside the car.

1. Are the seats in good shape? Look at the seat material. Is it ripped, soiled, or otherwise undesirable? Does the padding look deformed? Was the previous owner extremely heavy, making the seat unusable for you?

2. Sit in the seat and close the doors. Close your eyes and inhale. Do you get a good feeling, or do you feel uneasy?

3. Sit in the back seats. Check the seating material and details in the back.

4. How is the odor? Is there residual odor of abuse (vomit, beer, solvents, etc.). If you are a non-smoker and the seller smoked heavily, this may be a deterrent to you. You might use this as a negotiating point. You can always bargain for the money needed to get a good detailing job done to remove odors. Do this only if the odor is bearable, as there is no guarantee that detailing will take care of the problem.

5. Look for wear and tear that is not consistent with the mileage on the car. Torn seats or very worn pedals and armrests on a car that shows 32,000 miles is an indication that perhaps the mileage has been altered.

6. Do the window cranks or power windows work?

7. Check the lights and turn signals with someone on the outside. Also check the horn. If only you and the seller are present, ask him/her to try the signals while you check them from the outside.

8. Do the window wipers/washers work? Check front and back.

9. Do the seats move smoothly and easily?

10. Does the radio work? Check all the speakers. Note the stations that are fixed in memory. If it is a Spanish station and the seller is not, ask (again) if he is a dealer and not the original owner.

11. Start the engine and turn on the air conditioning. It should run cold. If not, assume the worst, repairing a frozen compressor will cost at least $500. Make sure the fan runs. If you know what you are doing, check to see if the compressor is frozen or if it is something simple like a broken belt.

12. Do all of the interior panels light up? Do all of the interior lights work? Are all the plastic covers in place?

13. Is the dashboard in good condition?

14. Is the steering wheel bent? This may indicate an accident.

15. With the car in park (neutral for a stick shift) run the engine very high for five seconds and notice what comes out the tailpipe. Be ready to walk away if the smoke is heavy white or blue. An initial transient blue puff of smoke on a car that has been sitting for a long while may indicate a valve seal problem.

16. Are there any missing small parts? Check knobs, window cranks, ashtray covers, etc.

17. Ask about the mileage again. Is this the original mileage or has the odometer been replaced or altered? If you have any doubts, have them guarantee the validity of the odometer reading in writing.

18. Look in the glove box for the manual, recent repair bills, etc. Ask what has been done to the car recently.

This is the easy part for most buyers. Most of us feel competent to inspect the inside and the outside easily, there is no mystique here, no hidden frammis gauge or transverse Fitzwalter clutch assembly. What is required here is a good eye and an attention to detail, not sophisticated technical knowledge. Now for the hard part: evaluating the mechanical integrity of the vehicle.

Mechanical

These are things you can check even if you are not a professional mechanic. If you spot something that may be indicative of trouble, you will be able to ask your mechanic about it.

1. Check the oil. If it is brand new, you learn nothing except that the seller had the oil changed to enhance the selling chances.

2. Look for a gelatinous goop around the inside of the oil fill cap or in the oil chamber. This may indicate a water leak. Be prepared to walk away at this point. Hard-caked muddy oil on a dipstick indicates that the oil in the past may not have been changed frequently. If the present oil is clean but the cap is muddy, the oil was changed to cover up the problem. When inspecting the oil, look for metal flakes or grit in the oil. If any are observed, be concerned.

3. Look for evidence of oil leakage on engine surfaces. Ask where the car is normally parked and look for oil there. You will need a mechanic to evaluate if it is serious. With the car in park and the idle low, look at the pressure gauge: if the oil pressure is low there may be an oil pump problem.

4. Look for fluid leaking onto such items as brakes, etc.

5. Check the radiator water. See if the antifreeze is new or if it is rust colored.

6. *If* the car has been sitting and is not hot, run your fingers around the inside of the tailpipe and see what comes out on them. If it is carbon and water, you are okay (maybe you need a tuneup). If it is oily, be careful. Do not put your fingers *near* the tailpipe if the car has been running; it gets very hot.

7. Check the belts and see if they are tight. If they look frayed or the edges are white, you may have some work to do.

8. Listen for noises. The engine should start and run quietly; if there is too much engine vibration there may be problems. A tapping or banging sound spells trouble. Any spraying of oil or water is bad news.

9. Check out the gears. All of them (forward and reverse) should work, and they should shift quietly. Check for pickup and power.

10. Check the transmission fluid. It should be pink. If it is yellow or brown and smells burnt, take it as evidence of major transmission problems.
11. With the car in drive, use the lowest amount of gas and see if the transmission slips.
12. At speed, slam on the brakes (warn your passenger first) and see how the car stops. There should be no squeaking and the vehicle should stop quickly in a straight line. Any bumping indicates the brakes are about shot. If the vehicle pulls strongly to one side, a brake job will be necessary soon.

This list is by no means complete, but it should get you through the initial evaluation of the vehicles soundness.

Negotiating Points

In your inspection of the car's exterior, interior, and mechanical soundness, you should also be on the lookout for peripheral information that will help you negotiate for a better price. The list below contains information you should collect that will help you in your price negotiations.

1. Repair work that has to be done.
2. Tires that have to be replaced.
3. Alignment or balancing that must be done.
4. Door dings or paint imperfections that must be corrected.
5. Seats that must be reupholstered.
6. Carpeting rips.
7. Replacement of missing knobs, bulbs, parts, etc.
8. Was the car in a fender bender or worse?
9. What kind of repair work or general maintenance has been done on the car?
10. Who has been driving the car — a kid, an older person?
11. Mileage and perhaps mileage discrepancies.

It is very legitimate to ask for price reductions to compensate for defects. Make sure that you compile a list during your inspection. It will prove invaluable when you begin negotiations with the seller.

22

Buying a Used Car from a Private Party

Selling is hard work for professional salespeople with resources, training, and all the other advantages outlined in earlier chapters. Selling is tough when you are a professional selling to a novice. Selling is tougher when you are a professional selling to a competent buyer. Selling is hardest for an untrained salesperson who doesn't like to sell and who is uncomfortable selling a car whose faults he knows. When you buy a car from an untrained private party, not only is he uncomfortable selling his vehicle, he most likely doesn't have the stomach for negotiation, much less a confrontation.

The amateur seller doesn't really know why his vehicle isn't selling. Is it the price? Are people detecting the flaws he tried so hard to hide? Is it the mileage? The color? Why won't they just say what they want and make life easier for him? He doesn't like to talk money and is visibly upset because the last few customers made an appointment and never showed up. He is tired of showing the car to people; tired of being insulted; tired of being hassled; and just wants to get the whole deal over with as soon as possible. He doesn't know what to do except lower the price until it sells and he is reluctant to do that. What usually happens is that he holds to his price, loses customer after customer, and when the tension level gets too high for him to handle any more, he just gives the car away to a good negotiator.

PRE-NEGOTIATION TACTICS

In order to even consider negotiating, you need to have a feel for the seller. In addition, you need to have the answers to some of the key questions mentioned in the previous chapter. One of the least painful ways to gain information is by making small talk.

Make some small talk to determine what kind of a person you are dealing with. Determine the following during small talk.

Small Talk Checklist

1. Is he the real seller?
2. Why is he selling the vehicle?
3. Is he comfortable selling the vehicle?
4. What does he need from this transaction?
5. How long has he been trying to sell this vehicle?
6. What is his real bottom line?
7. What can you trade off to get a better price?
8. Does he own the car, or does a bank or finance company?
9. Does he need to sell the car quickly to get money for a new vehicle?
10. Is he the type who can handle the sale and continually negotiate without getting his feelings bent out of shape?

Once you feel comfortable with the answers to these questions, shift to discussion of the vehicle itself. There are several questions that you can have him answer, still in the guise of small talk.

Discussion of the Vehicle

As a buyer it is your job to lead the other party into talking about the car: how it performs mechanically, what works and what doesn't, etc. Some helpful information to request includes:

1. Whether or not the car has ever been in an accident and fixed up.
2. Ask to see repair records.
3. Ask about gas mileage.
4. If you have looked up this car in *Consumer Reports* and know what types of defects are typical for this type of car, ask specifically if these repairs have ever been necessary.
5. Ask when the brakes were last done.
6. Ask when the oil and filter were last changed.
7. Ask when was the car was last lubed.

Every negative response further decreases the value of the car in his own estimation.

Look Like a Real Buyer

Although you are not buying a car from a professional car dealer, it is still crucial that you establish yourself as a real honest-to-goodness buyer. If you are perceived as a real buyer with real money, the seller will put up with a lot of aggravation to make the sale, unload his beloved car, and get back to a normal life.

We have already covered how to appear like a real buyer to a professional salesperson. The key points include saying, "I really want to buy a car today," appearing solvent, having a trade-in *ready*, and spending time with the salesperson.

Obviously, the professional salesperson is trained to pick up on all of these cues. How do you impress on a private party that you are a serious buyer for his car?

Let's look at some cues that he will easily understand:

♦ Flash some cash. Let the seller see that you have enough cash on your person for a down payment. The visual presence of cold cash is a very strong sign that you are serious about making a purchase immediately. My son, Andrew, and I do this easily because we are both 6'2" and 230 plus pounds. Make sure that you use common sense. Don't flash cash in "bad" neighborhoods, or potentially dangerous situations. (In fact, don't even go alone to "bad" neighborhoods or potentially dangerous situations.) Women will have to be especially careful regarding the safety of such a move.

♦ Indicate that you have been shopping a long time. Tell him about other vehicles you have seen and their faults. Create examples if necessary. Tell him that you really want to buy a vehicle soon — *if* you can get the right car at the right price.

♦ Inspect the vehicle carefully. Don't talk money until you have seen the vehicle, carefully inspected it, and gone for a test drive. If the vehicle is obviously not what you want, walk away. If the vehicle is suitable, take your time for a careful inspection as outlined in the previous chapter.

♦ Establish seller's ownership of car. Although we discussed this earlier, it cannot be overemphasized. Remember, when you are buying from a private party, you don't have the same guarantees of ownership that you have when buying from a licensed dealership. When responding to an ad by a private party, you have to be sure that you are not buying a stolen car, a car that has had its miles turned back, or a car that has been wrecked and then fixed up. Ask to see the title, and inspect it carefully. Look for erasures or additions of data. Also question it if something just doesn't make sense.

Ask the seller for his address, phone number, and driver's license number. If he gets upset about these requests, be cautious. You are about to spend money on something that you assume you will own. Make sure that the person selling the car has the legal right to sell it. You are entitled to request and receive any information necessary to make sure that the seller is the current owner. If he won't supply that information, assume the worst and walk away.

Make sure the VIN (Vehicle Identification Number) on the title matches the VIN on the vehicle. Make sure the vehicle description on the title matches the car. In short, make sure you are buying what you think you are buying.

Inquire if any liens on the car have been signed off. If necessary, get a verification from the lienholder that the loan has been paid off. A call to the party listed as lienholder will provide you with sufficient verification.

♦   Either bring a mechanic with you or take the car to a mechanic. Nothing makes you look as serious as having a mechanic with you.

♦   Ask questions. Ask lots of questions, find out why he is selling the car, how long it has been for sale, what works and doesn't, if he has had a lot of interest, etc. When asking questions, see what the other party doesn't respond to comfortably. Take notes; nothing makes a person trying to hide a problem squirm like a note taker. If you are writing down information, you must be a serious buyer.

Okay, now you have inspected the car and established to the owner's satisfaction that you are his white knight, a real buyer. Now what do you do?

NEGOTIATION

Create Tension

This is very difficult for most of us. We are nice people who spend our lives smoothing ruffled feathers, not intentionally ruffling them. But here, your prime objective is to get the best price possible. In order to do this, you must create tension that he will want to relieve, hopefully by lowering the price. Your job is to create tension and make the seller relieve it by giving in to you on price or some other issue.

You don't create tension by agreeing, by being empathetic, or by giving the other person an easy reason to dismiss you. Make it an easy decision for the seller to do what you need him to do and difficult for him to do otherwise.

All of us are up to our eyeballs in stress. We have kids who are sick, spouses who are stressed, and bosses who yell. We have impending deadlines, laundry to pick up, dogs at the vet, *and* we have to sell this stupid car because we can't afford the payments on the new truck.

If we *don't* have a high stress level, we feel guilty because we are not utilizing our time effectively. So we take courses in how to pack more into our days, we get organizers, beepers, and cellular phones, hire maids, gardeners, and secretaries, and then start to delegate to anyone who makes eye contact. The guilt also produces stress. We now feel stressed because we feel guilty because we are not stressed enough.

Eventually the stress gets so high we can't handle it anymore and we have to do something to end it. Perhaps we just have to give up and get rid of that old car.

The essence of good negotiation is finding a common ground and negotiating a win/win solution. Developing a relationship where you and the person from whom you bought the car will live happily ever after in mutual love, respect, harmony, peace, and tranquility. However, to gain that love, respect, harmony, peace, and tranquility, you will have to give up some money. With that money you can buy a vacation in the Bahamas and for a week or two find tranquility, peace, harmony, respect, and if you are really lucky, love.

The point here is to try to get the very best deal you can. I call this type of car-buying transaction a "Commando Raid." This is my name for a one-time transaction where neither party will ever meet with the other again and where cutthroat tactics are appropriate. This is not the time to build up trust for future transactions. You won't see or negotiate with the other party again and a typical win/win transaction doesn't really make sense because there is only one issue to be decided: *price*. You want the most you can possibly get for your money.

When you deal with your spouse, interact with your boss, or trade favors with your neighbors, you know you will see and/or work with these people again. You will probably *never* see this stranger again after you buy his car. Even if you are a nice person who treats everybody fairly, how do you know that this stranger will treat you fairly, or that his car is really as good as he says? I am not suggesting that you cheat the seller, only that you get the best possible deal for yourself, and make sure that he doesn't cheat you.

Now with the morality of creating tension out of the way, let's see how to create tension in the other party that you can then help solve to your advantage.

Don't Be the First to Mention Money

As a buyer of a vehicle, the longer you can delay mentioning what you want to pay for the vehicle, the better your chances of getting a lower price from the seller. Get the other party to talk money before he fully talks about the virtues of his vehicle. If he mentions a price and you ignore his offer and go on to other details, he may cut his own price trying to get an offer or some expression of interest from you. He is lowering his own tension level. Create tension for him to relieve.

Learn to Flinch on Command

I know this sounds strange, but when somebody mentions money to you, it is to your great advantage to flinch. Practice it so that when somebody mentions a price you will twitch or jerk — seemingly spontaneously—and say something like, "Really, that doesn't seem like such a good price." The person mentioning price will question the validity of his statement. They may think, "Wow, this price must be way off." They then feel that they must do something so as not to loose this valuable customer. They may immediately say something like, "Oh, excuse me did I say the car cost $4900? I meant to say $4650, no wonder you jumped." At least give him a chance to change his own bid before you mention a price. Watch professional car dealers, they have flinching down to a fine art.

If a flinch means, "I don't like the figure," then the lack of a flinch when somebody mentions price is a tacit acceptance of a figure. The person who gives you the figure thinks to himself, "That price must be close; she didn't even bat an eyelash." *Always* flinch. It won't ruin your dignity and it may help you keep a bit more wealth.

Responding to an Offer

To review this point, let's look at how you can mentally rephrase his first offer so that you do not hear it as a take it or leave it offer. We covered this in the section on new cars. If the seller says, "I will sell you my beautiful Ford Taurus for $4900," mentally rephrase it to sound like, "My initial price is no more than $4900 and you can probably talk me down." If you rephrase his offer in these terms it is less difficult to counter his bid.

Remember, each time you are given a price, flinch and then rephrase the offer in your own mind so that you can respond to it better.

Also, don't feel it is necessary to answer a person's offer directly. Many times it is to your advantage to skirt the issue of price rather than going head to head with the seller. For instance, if the seller says, "I will sell you my beautiful Ford Taurus for $4900," you could respond directly by saying, "I don't want to pay any more than $3850 for it." This will create a reaction of dismay and a lowering of goals (both good for you) in the seller. In addition, he may possibly show irritation because you seem to be playing with his mind (not so great). This is one way to start a cat fight over price.

A more productive response to his initial offer of $4900 would be to flinch, then respond indirectly by saying, "It is a nice vehicle, but before we discuss price, let's discuss how much it will cost to fix the knock in the engine." The seller is going to feel an increase in pressure because he mentioned price and you did not respond directly. He wants you to counter-offer so that he can settle the matter. He also intuitively knows that a detailed discussion of the car's faults is going to lower the price.

The indirect response changes the subject and subtly indicates that $4900 is unacceptable without offering an alternative. This increases the tension for the seller. He knows that he will have to compromise on the price since his $4900 is marred by a mechanical problem. What will happen next is that the knocking problem will be solved by the seller indicating that he doesn't think it is serious. He will probably offer to give you a couple of hundred dollars off for mechanical repairs — if you settle for $4700.

He wants to settle right away. Your best response to this second offer is another indirect response. Say something like, "Great, that takes care of the knocking problem. Now, what are you going to do about this broken power window? Will you pay to have it fixed?" Your best response is to tacitly accept his concession and move on to other problems on the vehicle without giving any concessions of your own. Do this as long as you can.

The world's great chess players use the creation of stress to their advantage. They know that people have different levels of tolerance for stress and many of them developed very intricate games which would try the patience of lesser chess players. At some point, the pressure and stress of playing an intricate chess game forces these lesser players to make a mistake or to try to relieve the stress by making a daring and unsound move.

Don't Give the Seller an Easy Out

The easiest way to end a "Commando Raid" is for the raided party to find some easy way not to deal with you. For instance, if you insult the other party, he can easily — and rightly — ask you to leave. Thus he relieves the immediate stress, but of course it doesn't settle his long-term stress of having to sell his car. Always be polite, forceful, and aware of the fact that you are the customer and you have the money so you can call some of the shots.

Don't Be Over Friendly or Too Nice

This is not a social event, and people tend to push really nice people around. Your attitude should make him just a little uneasy. He should know that if he tries to jerk you around he will lose the sale. Take command, act offended if it helps your cause, be a little flaky and excitable. Good acting skills are a big plus.

Control the Agenda

Make him stick to your important points. Many people don't like to dwell on the difficult points immediately. The seller will try to build the car up in your eyes so that any potential problems seem minor in comparison to the great car there in front of you. Sellers will circle around the bad points and will get to the vital issues only if forced. Your job is to focus your attention and questions on the things he avoids. This helps you in several ways: it begins to devalue the car in his eyes, thus making a price reduction more likely; it keeps his tension level high, thus making him want to relieve it; and it keeps the conversation going where *you* want it to, not where *he* wants it to.

The following scenario puts this together in an easy to emulate example.

SELLER: Nice car, huh? I am only asking $5950 for it.

YOU: The car is certainly usable. But what are you going to do about allowing a mechanic's inspection and giving me a fifteen-day guarantee on the car?

SELLER: I hadn't really thought about a fifteen-day guarantee. I've never heard of anyone doing that before. Why don't I just drop the price to $5750?

YOU: $5750 is certainly a more realistic price, but let's concentrate on the mechanic's inspection and the guarantee, shall we?

NOTE: You have accepted his price reduction without giving anything in exchange and now are focusing on the two issues you want to discuss. If this discussion goes on long enough, say ten minutes or more, the seller will forget that he ever asked for $5950, will accept the $5750 price, and may be amenable to another price reduction if you drop the guarantee issue.

SELLER: Okay, if you give up the guarantee issue, I will let you take the car to your mechanic and I will lower the price by $250 to $5700. Okay?

YOU (flinching): I will accept a $250 price reduction for dropping the guarantee requirement, even though I am worried about the drive train, but we had been talking about a $250 reduction from the last price of $5750, right? We haven't discussed the $5950 price since I first got here.

SELLER (Possibly confused, afraid he will lose the sale, and noting that the amount is not huge): I *was* talking about the original figure, but it is obvious you weren't. If we can just settle on this number and do it now, I will settle for $5450.

YOU: Okay then, that solves the guarantee issue. Just one more small thing and then we can settle the price.

REMEMBER, nothing gets resolved, the tension on the seller is not relieved, until *you*, the buyer, resolve it.

Give Him a Take It or Leave It Offer

As mentioned before, this is the way we have been trained to think about financial transactions. This is the main negotiating philosophy in the good old U. S. of A. It is promulgated by the way we automatically buy things without negotiating. Apples are 59 cents a pound: if you don't want to pay the price, go somewhere else. However, you usually have more options than to take it or leave it. If an offer is halfway decent, the average American feels that he has to react — to either take or leave the offer. As I've said before, try to hear offers as a starting point and resist a take it or leave it offer when given to you. In addition, you should try experimenting with giving a take it or leave it offer to the selling party. Who knows, they may just take it.

If you have decided that you want the car at the right price, now is the time to do something about it. I guarantee that if as a buyer you are a little uneasy and uncertain about how to jump into it, then the seller, especially if he is a first time seller, is feeling even worse.

There are ways to tell if you are dealing with an experienced seller. If the seller does any of these things, you can bet this is not his first sale.
1. Uses techniques previously discussed on you
2. Has a dealer's license on one of his other cars
3. Is a dealer
4. Has more than one car for sale
5. Asks a lot of questions of you
6. Is constantly trying to build rapport with you
7. Is constantly closing on you for a commitment to buy
8. Somehow or other you feel that the seller is in control

On the other hand, the following are indicative of an inexperienced salesperson. If the seller does these things, you can be pretty sure he/she is inexperienced.
1. Keeps saying "honestly" or "truthfully"
2. Doesn't seem to know how to ask for the sale
3. Doesn't use any of the tactics you saw earlier
4. Talks all the time rather than asking you what you need or what is important
5. Gives way on price easily when you voice an objection
6. Looks embarrassed when negotiating

As mentioned above, you want the seller to be the first to tell you how much money he wants. This is even better if he has given way on some issues before the first price is mentioned.

If you are ready to make an offer, a good lead-in based on the above scenario would be:

I would now like to talk seriously about buying your car. It seems that we have resolved the knock in the engine and the power window problems, and that was after you gave me your bottom price of $5450. I must tell you that I like the vehicle and I like you personally, and feel you are a fair and honorable person, and I want to buy the car today. However, I feel the price is too high. Can you help me on that some more? What is your best price for the vehicle if I buy it right now?

NOTE: Make sure that you are *very* nice at this point. Prior to starting a serious negotiation, it is useful to compliment the person you are dealing with so as not to give him a reason for dismissing your low bid (and it will be low) and relieving the tension on him because he thinks you are insulting him or playing with his mind.

By mentioning the defects in the car and the resolution of issues after a bottom line price was mentioned, the stage is set for the seller to drop the price and to accept this lower price as his initial price in a negotiation.

As the negotiation proceeds, pick out some tactics that might work and try them. For instance, try the broken record and yes … but tactics and see how he handles it.

SELLER: I really think the car is worth $4550.

YOU: Yes, I know you like your vehicle and think it is a good price, but I think the car has some problems and I have to fix them.

SELLER: The fixup is minor, and won't cost more than $50. If we settle now I will drop to $4500.

YOU: Yes I am glad you will pay for the fixup, and I thank you for it, but $4500 is still very high.

You can also try the "you have to do better than that" tactic:

SELLER: I really think the car is worth $4500.

YOU: I would like to drive home in this vehicle today, but you really have to do better than that.

SELLER: What? How much better?

YOU: You have to do considerably better than that.

NOTE: If the seller doesn't react well to a particular tactic, try another one. One of them is bound to work.

Eventually you will agree on a price. Make sure that the car has a valid title and that the price is acceptable. Confirm that all the conditions have been agreed upon. Now is the time to trade your money for his car.

Just before the money changes hands, smile and act pleased. Say that you know you will love the car and that he drives a hard bargain.

23

Selling Your Own Car

Now that we have looked at how you can get the best deal for yourself as the buyer of a used car, let's turn the situation around. How do you go about getting the best deal for yourself as the *seller* of a used car? If you think you can get more for your trade-in by selling it as a private party then you ought to try. If you use this threat on the car salesperson and he calls your bluff, you may well find it necessary to do so. It has been my experience that you may be able to make considerably more money by selling your own car than by trading it in. You will find out, however, that it is not always an easy thing to do. There are advantages and disadvantages to selling your own car. First, let's look at the disadvantages.

DISADVANTAGES

♦ Safety. Most single women would not want to go for test drives — a necessary part of the selling procedure — with strange men. This can be easily remedied if you can enlist a friend (male or female) to join you. There is a certain safety in numbers. Choose a friend who is not going to be a liability — someone who can just be a silent presence and not become involved in the negotiations or small talk.

♦ Time. It takes a lot of time to sell a car. You have to place ads, and then stay home and wait for phone calls. You have to show the car to people at *their* convenience, and you can kill a lot of weekends waiting for people to show up and view your vehicle. Many individuals work unusual hours and want to see the car at strange times.

♦ Loss of privacy. People will call at strange hours. Others who have seen the car may drop by unexpectedly to show it to someone else.

♦ No shows. A lot of people will make appointments to see your vehicle and then not show up and you will never know why.

♦ General hassles. A lot of people will pick the car to death for problems and then ask for a huge price reduction on the car. Some people will demand extensive repairs or require you to fix certain things (usually for free) before they will buy your car. Others will haggle endlessly to get what they want. People want guarantees, repair receipts, etc.

♦ Dealers. Dealers make ridiculous offers just to get the car cheaply.

♦ Curiosity seekers. You will get a lot of traffic from people who are just checking out the cars on sale, or who are at the beginning of their car-buying process and are not really serious buyers.

♦ Money is always a problem and some people may want or need you to help finance the car for them, take a trade-in, do a barter arrange-ment, or some other deal that does not involve a cash transaction. These situations should be avoided. You want to receive the money from the buyer and not have to create a long relationship in order to get rid of your car.

♦ Stress. The selling experience may be stressful to you because selling does not come easily to you; you are just not a natural salesperson.

If you decide to sell your own car and the problems just outlined are not a major factor, let's go ahead and look at the process. Obviously, your first step is to place your ad in the paper and wait for the calls to start coming in. You can, of course, just babble on and perhaps luck into an easy sale, but that doesn't always happen. In order to maximize your return from your vehicle, you need a strategy for answering query calls.

FIELDING PHONE RESPONSES

The purpose of spending time on the phone with potential buyers is twofold: you want to weed out those people who are not serious buyers; you want to get as many serious buyers as possible to see the car. There are several things you can do to assist yourself in this process. The first thing to do is to be comfortable with selling your car. Practice your sales pitch in front of a mirror or with another person (or a tape recorder) until you feel comfortable with it.

Questions to Ask

♦ Get all caller's names, addresses, and phone numbers. Don't go any further without this information. It protects you and screens out non-buyers. It also allows you to call people back if they miss an appointment or if you will be late.

♦ Don't allow yourself to be interrogated by the potential buyer. An interrogation is where they ask all the questions and you do nothing but answer. You want to ask questions as well as answer them.

♦ Always tell the other party that the car is great, that it shows well and has no problems. Save the problems for a face-to-face contact. Your telephone job is to get the customers down to see the car, not to describe the vehicle in detail.

♦ Say, "You will love the car, the paint (or something else) is really nice." Let the caller know it is a great car and that you hate to sell it.

♦ Have a viable reason for selling the car. Create one if necessary. Some good reasons are, "My son went to college and I am selling his car," or, "We need a bigger/smaller car and I wanted to trade it in but the new car dealer wouldn't give me a fair price." Never indicate that you are selling the car because you are going bankrupt or because the car is giving you mechanical difficulties.

♦ Find out who the car is for and what they need. Try to meet this need.

♦ Tell every caller that your car has gotten a lot of attention and is in great demand so they ought to see it right away. Talk about other people coming to see it. If this isn't happening the first time you say it, it will be by the second or third.

♦ Find out if the caller needs a car right away. In other words, ask callers if they are real buyers.

♦ Don't discuss price over the phone. Let them know that if they come to see the car and are interested and want to buy it, you are sure you can reach a mutually agreeable price.

♦ Schedule potential buyers close together in time so it looks as if the car is in great demand.

Questions to Expect

Have a check sheet handy that lists and describes all the features of the auto. Be prepared to answer the following questions:

Q. How long have you owned the car?
A. The ideal answer is, "I am the original owner." Even if you are not, it is the ideal answer, but you should be honest.

Q. How much are you asking for the car?
A. Do not answer this with a number. Instead, ask them if they are prepared to make an offer. Ask if they will have a down payment with them. Ask if they are serious buyers. Ask them if they saw the ad in the paper. Get them to make a first bid.

Q. What's wrong with the car?
A. Don't disclose everything immediately. You can build confidence by indicating something small, like the radio has a loose wire. Don't get caught in a fit of excessive honesty; don't answer questions that aren't asked and don't volunteer more than required. Once they see the car and have become attached to the idea of buying it, you can answer more directly while pointing out assets to counter the faults.

Q. How long has the car been for sale?
A. Don't answer with a number of days, weeks, etc. Indicate that it hasn't

been for sale too long and that you have been getting a lot of action on the ad. Remember to tell them that it looks like your car is pretty hot.

Q. Don't these cars have a lot of problems?

A. This car has had only the normal sorts of problems and repairs. Don't volunteer information on major problems over the phone. You may scare away potential buyers.

Q. Has the car ever been in an accident?

A. If the answer is yes, minimize the impact by answering indirectly. Say, "The bumper and fender have been replaced and the car now looks immaculate and drives perfectly."

Q. Is this the original mileage or has the odometer ever been turned back?

A. Yes is the only correct answer. You should never tamper with the odometer.

FACE TO FACE

Selling your trade-in to a professional as part of a new car buy presents one series of problems. Selling your car to a private party presents quite another. You are the true salesperson in the latter case and have the salesperson's advantages. Here are some tips to use as a salesperson to help you sell your car.

♦ One of your key responsibilities as a salesperson is to qualify the potential buyer. Ask if he has a down payment with him. Look to see if he can afford the car. See if he is serious before you spend a lot of time and energy negotiating. If the buyer is not serious, doesn't have the money, or is just trying to grind you down, decide if you want to string him along, get rid of him, or really need his business.

♦ Be pleasant, yet a little reserved.

♦ Have records handy. Be prepared to show your title, repair bills, and any other documentation that will help convince potential buyers that this is the car for them.

♦ Remain in control of the situation. Remember to ask questions rather than being interrogated.

♦ If forced, give a price that is realistic but that will give you $200 to $300 bargaining room.

♦ Give way grudgingly on price or other details. When making concessions, make smaller ones than they do, and act as if you are nearing the end of the line.

♦ When you feel that he has been given enough information to make a decision, ask directly if he is interested and what he needs to make a decision to buy the car today.

Final Negotiating Points

Negotiating is tough, especially if you are not used to negotiating, not strong enough to stand up to forceful personalities, or intimidated by the whole process of selling a car for the first time. When you are trying to settle a price with a serious buyer, several of the sales techniques that I warned you about earlier can be used to your advantage here.

♦ First, ask the buyer "Are you prepared to buy now?" That will indicate if the other party is a real buyer. Then ask follow-up questions, including: What is important to you in the purchase of a used car? What do you need to buy now? When you find out what he needs, try to supply it. Find his hot button.

♦ Tell the buyer only what he needs to know, no more, no less, and slant it to your best advantage. (Surely you remember doing this on first dates.) Answer only the questions that are asked and do not volunteer information — especially harmful information.

♦ Play dumb if it helps you. Responding with, "I'm not sure," or "I just don't understand," can put off a major question/answer session.

♦ If your original asking price is $4900, indicate to the buyer that you have already turned down $4200 — even if you haven't. This will prevent his making a ridiculously low offer.

♦ When tempted to accept an offer, compare it to the offer given to you by the dealership. Don't panic into an acceptance. If it is considerably above the dealership offer, consider taking it rather than haggling endlessly and risking letting the sale slip away.

♦ If the buyer wants to have his mechanic inspect the car, offer to pay for it *if* he buys the car. If the inspection is good, you will pay for it, but he must put down money and commit. Indicate that if the inspection is *not* satisfactory, you will not pay for it, but that you are confident the car will pass. This usually prevents a person from demanding a mechanical inspection unless he or she is very serious about buying the car.

♦ If more than one person comes to inspect the car, find out who will use the car, who has the money, and who is making the final decision. Your job is to make the person who will drive the vehicle love it, to show the money person that everything is legit and that the price is right, and to convince the decision maker to say yes. Compartmentalize your discussion. Discuss color, etc. with the one who will drive the car. If one of the people is a pain, ignore him if you can. They may be playing a game with you.

Armed with these techniques, you should do very well against all but the most experienced car buyers.

24

Special Concerns of Women

CREATING TENSION

One of the very best books I have read recently is Deborah Tannen's *You Just Don't Understand* (Ballantine, 1990). This best-selling book provided me with great insights into the differences between the thinking processes and communication styles of men and women. While this is not a psychology book, I think that this information will help women understand why negotiation has not been easy for them and will teach them a new style that is more appropriate for car buying.

Tannen focuses on the impact that same-sex communication in the formative years has on the style of interaction we carry with us into our adult years. As a generalization, males tend to play hard and to compete in groups while females tend to be more cooperative. Both groups negotiate differently; males to win, females to cooperate. These different negotiating methods present different problems for each gender. Unfortunately for the women, the "male" style of negotiation is the one most frequently encountered. Buying a car or a house requires the competitive, male style of negotiation.

Earlier, I talked about the "Commando Raid" (a one-time transaction where neither party will ever meet with the other again and where cutthroat tactics are appropriate). According to both Tannen's definition and my conversations with women, this type of negotiation is particularly difficult for most women. It just goes against their "grain." Obviously, there are some women for whom hard negotiation is easy and some males for whom it seems impossible. This information is by necessity a generalization.

One of the key ingredients in successful negotiating is the creation of tension. As a rule, this is difficult for women to do. They are trained to ease tension, not to create it. I illustrate this in the classes I teach on "How to Buy a Car." I try to help students hone their negotiating skills, including their ability to create tension. As a preliminary exercise, I choose a male from the audience and strongly criticize his appearance and apparel. I make terrible comments about his clothes, his fashion sense, and finally, his posture. Then I invite any woman in the class to do the same thing to any other woman in the class. I explain that everyone knows that it is just an exercise and that the volunteer can apologize in advance. I even tell her to explain that she is just doing the exercise to show up a chauvinistic, egoistic, obnoxious male. I have never had a taker. This is just the type of attack necessary for a "Commando Raid."

In addition to the difficulty women have in creating tension, there are six primary trouble spots for women in using a "Commando Raid". These are: physical safety, win-lose situations, product knowledge, victim status, required forcefulness, and direct confrontation.

PHYSICAL SAFETY

Problem

In some car-buying situations, fear for physical safety is a factor. As mentioned elsewhere, I often car shop with my son Andrew. Both of us are 6'2" and over 230 pounds. We do not feel threatened carrying cash and going into a stranger's house to negotiate over price. I also don't feel threatened when going for test drives with people I don't know. I will often get calls from female acquaintances asking me to accompany them and a male customer for their used car. Unfortunately, security has to be a priority in the mind of the female.

As a result, it is more threatening and difficult for single women to sell their cars themselves. Test drives are not the only discomforting possibility, many women are understandably reluctant to give out their names and addresses to people they do not know. Women's safety concerns are realistic in the world as we know it.

Solution

Those women who do decide to sell their cars themselves are already at a disadvantage if they are physically intimidated by male customers. While it makes the process a bit more cumbersome, I suggest that single women who choose to sell their used cars arrange to have friends go with them on test drives and/or be in the house when potential buyers arrive.

WIN-LOSE SITUATIONS

Problem

It is particularly difficult for women to negotiate in a way that isn't "nice" to the opposing negotiator. In car buying, there is no long-term friendship to cement, no reason to make the car seller like you. Once the transaction is over, you will, in all likelihood, never see this person again. As Tannen stresses, women work to create connection. This is in direct opposition to the tactics required to win in a car negotiation.

Solution

Mental preparation is the key here. You must be prepared to drive a killer deal. This is done by collecting information during the negotiation. This is actually easier for women than for men. According to Tannen, women are better at opening conversations and asking questions. One key to getting a big win is to ask for it. Ask, ask, ask. Don't be shy or beat around the bush.

PRODUCT KNOWLEDGE

Problem

As a rule, many women are at a great disadvantage in car-buying or selling situations because of their lack of auto knowledge. Many men don't know a fuel injector from a valve lifter anymore than do most women. Yet, in order to evaluate a new or used vehicle, you must be able to put a value on the vehicle. This presents a problem to all buyers, but it is more of a problem for women than it is for men. Most men have had more conversations about car value, etc., than have most women.

Solution

Remember the section on homework? This section is of paramount importance to women looking for a car. The more research you have done into your particular automobile, the less easily you will be confused or intimidated — or dismissed — by a professional car salesman.

Having said that, let me stress that it isn't enough. You must at least appear marginally knowledgeable on the mechanics of the car as well — especially for used car purchases. There is a lot more negotiating power available to you if you have checked the exhaust for black soot and checked the condition of the oil and can combine that information with the research you have done. To tell a seller that his car is not only rated poorly, but has obvious mechanical problems beyond those concerns, is going to devalue his car in his eyes.

If you do not possess enough product knowledge by the time you go to look for a car, take along someone who can help you. It is to your advantage to pay a mechanic to look at a vehicle. Not only can the mechanic locate any problems and put your mind at ease, the threat of a real expert examining the car is sometimes enough to intimidate a seller into coming down on price. If you are selling your car, pay a garage to inspect your car carefully and provide an itemized checklist to present to potential buyers. Get any help you can. Remember that you can compensate for any deficiencies you have by utilizing the expertise of those around you. It is not important that you know everything, just that you know how to find the answers to any questions you might have.

VICTIM STATUS

Problem

Claiming victim status has become a great negotiating ploy of the '80s and '90s. The car salesperson knows this and will try to use it on you (I have to sell x number of cars this week or I may lose my job because my boss is so unfair . . .) but it will not work on him. If you appear weaker, you will not get a better or fairer deal, you will lose the respect of the dealer and he may well treat you like a victim.

Solution

There is no way that you can "guilt" a car salesperson into giving you a fair deal. It just doesn't work that way. You must negotiate strongly and take charge. Otherwise, you will not get the deal you deserve.

REQUIRED FORCEFULNESS

Problem

In order to win in negotiating the best price for a car, you must be forceful and direct. One of the best tactics is to force or browbeat the other party into submission. Wear them out, beat them down, make them want to give in just to end the confrontation. These are not elegant tactics, but they work amazingly well. They also come much more naturally to men than to women.

Solution

These tactics only work if you can be convincing. If this makes you so uncomfortable that you cannot possibly pull it off, remember the other tactics covered in the book. Also, there are some people against whom they won't work at all. See what response you get from the opposing negotiator. Does he get defensive and hostile, or does he seem intimidated? If the tactics work, keep them up. If they don't, refer to the other tactics covered in the book.

DIRECT CONFRONTATION

Problem

Expect "Commando Raids" to be characterized by direct confrontation. Expect this from the other party and do not allow yourself to become intimidated. Money is at stake here for both the buyer and the seller. Be prepared to stand tough in the face of harsh directness on the part of the salesperson. Pay special attention to the advice on negotiating in this book. By being a strong force and resisting the temptation to give in to the pressure of the salesperson, you can get more car for your money.

Solution

You can counter the intimidating tactics of others in several ways. If they try to intimidate you by crowding your physical space, ask if there is someplace that you can sit down to negotiate. Then put some distance between you and the other party. Counter their fast-driving, intimidating forcefulness by slowing down the negotiations and going over things more slowly and thoroughly. Remember, stay in charge. If the salesperson is rude, remind him that it is your money, that you really want to buy a car today, and that you will take your money and your business elsewhere if he insists on being rude to you. Do not allow him to treat you like an inferior being — you are not. You are the customer and you are in charge, whether he knows it or not.

APPENDIX: CHECKLISTS

TYPE OF CAR NEEDED

This Car Will Be Used For:

_____ driving to work
_____ hauling cargo
_____ hauling kids and groceries
_____ impressing the neighbors
_____ improving better social life (sports car)
_____ long distance commuting
_____ sales calls
_____ other _____
_____ other _____
_____ other _____

I Need a Car with the Following Characteristics:

_____ lots of economy
_____ lots of luxury
_____ lots of power
_____ lots of room
_____ holds ___ people easily
_____ 2, 4, 5 doors
_____ other_____
_____ other_____
_____ other_____
_____ other_____

		WANT	NEED	COMMENTS (PRO/CON)
1.	luxury car	_____	_____	_____
2.	minivan	_____	_____	_____
3.	recreation vehicle	_____	_____	_____
4.	sedan 4-door	_____	_____	_____
5.	sedan 2-door	_____	_____	_____
6.	sports car	_____	_____	_____
7.	station wagon	_____	_____	_____
8.	truck	_____	_____	_____
9.	other	_____	_____	_____

CONCLUSIONS ABOUT WHAT KIND OF CAR I NEED:

_____

_____

LIST OF OPTIONS WANTED

FEATURE	SELECTION
Air conditioning	yes/no
Anti-lock brakes	yes/no
Anti-theft package	yes/no
Color	_____
Cruise control	yes/no
Doors (number)	2/3/4/5
Extended warranty	yes/no
Exterior protection packages	yes/no
Interior package	yes/no
Interior protection packages	yes/no
Life insurance	yes/no
Light package	yes/no
Motor size (number of cylinders)	4/6/8/12
Power features:	
♦ power seats	yes/no
♦ power mirrors	yes/no
♦ power windows	yes/no
♦ power doors	yes/no
Roof rack	yes/no
Rust protection	yes/no
Safety features: air bag, etc.	yes/no
Sound system (buy elsewhere?)	yes/no
Special features:	
♦ center console	yes/no
♦ other _____	yes/no
Suspension type	_____
Tilt wheel	yes/no
Top styles:	
♦ T-top	yes/no
♦ moon roof	yes/no
♦ convertible	yes/no
♦ hard top	yes/no
Towing package	yes/no
Transmission type	automatic/manual
Trim packages:	
♦ including special upholstery	yes/no
♦ exterior trim	yes/no
♦ leather	yes/no
♦ pockets	yes/no

♦   drink holders   yes/no
♦   other _____   yes/no
Type of seats   bench/bucket
Other specials _____   yes/no
(such as a still higher level sound system, CD players, etc.)

PRIORITY RATING CHARTS

CHARACTERISTIC	MY PRIORITIES	RATING BY EXPERTS
acceleration	_____	_____
braking	_____	_____
bumpers	_____	_____
controls	_____	_____
cost	_____	_____
displays	_____	_____
driving position	_____	_____
emergency handling	_____	_____
front seating	_____	_____
fun to drive	_____	_____
gas mileage	_____	_____
heating	_____	_____
noise	_____	_____
rear seating	_____	_____
reliability	_____	_____
ride	_____	_____
routine handling	_____	_____
servicing	_____	_____
towing capability	_____	_____
trunk	_____	_____
value	_____	_____
ventilation	_____	_____

Special Items Wanted:

ITEM	WANTED	RATING BY EXPERTS
air conditioning	yes/no	
cruise control	yes/no	_____
luxury package	yes/no	_____
moon roof	yes/no	_____
power brakes	yes/no	_____
power steering	yes/no	_____

ITEM	WANTED	RATING BY EXPERTS
roof rack	yes/no	_____
special engine	yes/no	_____
special exterior package	yes/no	_____
special interior package	yes/no	_____
special suspension	yes/no	_____
special tires	yes/no	_____
T-top	yes/no	_____
tilt steering	yes/no	_____
towing package	yes/no	_____
other_____	yes/no	_____
other_____	yes/no	_____
other_____	yes/no	_____

Special Recommendations of Experts

upgrade engine	yes/no
upgrade suspension	yes/no
upgrade transmission	yes/no
automatic or stick	_____
preferred model	_____
corporate twin available	yes/no
other_____	yes/no
other_____	yes/no

◆ Is the vehicle being considered a first-year design
   of uncertain reliability?   yes/no
◆ Do the experts say this is important?   yes/no
◆ Do the experts think the styling is dated?   yes/no
◆ Is this the last year the car will be produced?
   (like a Merkur or a Renault)   yes/no
◆ Is the vehicle in great demand?   yes/no

Final List

Now look over all the data you have gathered and list the cars (company and model) that fill the bill.

1. _____

2. _____

3. _____

4. _____

CALCULATING AFFORDABILITY

1. Maximum *total* price you can afford to pay $_____
2. Maximum monthly payment you can afford $_____
3. Realistic price for a suitable type vehicle $_____
4. What is your trade-in worth? $_____
5. How much cash can you put down? $_____
6. Taxes, licenses, and other fees $_____
7. Transportation cost $_____
8. Extended warranty and other extras $_____
9. Factory rebates $_____
10. Premiums, an AMU or an ADMU $_____
11. Options, extras, special tires, etc. $_____

Total to be Financed:

3 + 6 + 7 + 8 + 10 + 11 - 4 - 5 - 9 = $_____

CHECKING YOUR VEHICLE'S WORTH

$_____   Blue Book wholesale value
$_____   estimated value of options (+ or -)
$_____   estimated value of mileage (+ or -)

$_____   total wholesale value of car (base + options + mileage)

$_____   Blue Book base "retail" value
$_____   estimated value of options (+ or -)
$_____   estimated value of mileage (+ or -)

$_____   total retail value of car (base + options + mileage)

$_____   First Newspaper Price
$_____   Second Newspaper Price
$_____   Third Newspaper Price

$_____   Dealer's Buy Price
$_____   Dealer's Sell Price

$_____   Auction Price

THE PRE-DRIVE INSPECTION

♦ Do you love the exterior? If not, should you look at another vehicle.
♦ Do you love its interior ambiance, or is it just adequate?
♦ Are the doors so heavy or the door handles so awkward it is a strain to use them?
♦ Do the doorstops keep the door open easily?
♦ Can you lock and unlock the doors easily from the inside?
♦ Are you comfortable in the car? Do your feet fit the pedals?
♦ Test the seats in all positions. Can you get in and out of them easily? Are they adequately adjustable?
♦ Do the seats have good back support?
♦ Is the headrest adequately adjustable?
♦ Does your head hit the roof?
♦ Are the lights, wiper switches, cruise control, radio, etc., easy to find and use?
♦ Is the horn easily found and easy to use?
♦ Is the interior lighting adequate?
♦ Are there map lights? Do they work well?
♦ Will the lights automatically turn off when the engine shuts down?
♦ Can you easily read the gauges, radio, and computer readouts, both day and night?
♦ Are the controls usable or are they too complicated?
♦ Are both mirrors adjustable from the driver's side?
♦ Are there adequate pockets? For instance, where would you put a map, a book of maps, a pocketbook, your garage opener, extra keys, cigarettes, and other small items?
♦ Are there vanity mirrors on both visors of the car? Are they lit?
♦ Are there coin slots and cup holders?
♦ Is there a front seat console for tapes, CDs, etc.?
♦ Can you easily attach and adjust the seat belts?
♦ Can you easily see over the hood?
♦ Can you see over the back and front of the car?
♦ Can you easily see into the back seat to talk to others or watch your kids?
♦ Are there air bags on both sides?

THE MOVING INSPECTION

♦ Did the car start easily? Turn the car on and off several times.
♦ Is the steering column easy to lock and unlock?
♦ Does the radio work well? Is the sound adequate for you?
♦ Does the car maneuver easily at low speeds getting out of the lot?
♦ How is the turning radius? Can you make a U-turn in the road?
♦ Can you parallel park easily?
♦ How is the acceleration? Can you zip around in comfort and in control of the situation?
♦ Is there enough acceleration to easily fit into traffic — even freeway traffic? How about going up a hill?
♦ Is the car powerful enough? Does it pass easily? Does it have enough power to get up hills when loaded?
♦ Is there power at both low speeds and higher speeds? Many cars have drive trains that are fine at lower speeds and die at higher speeds.
♦ Is the car so big it feels like a boat, or so small it feels vulnerable?
♦ If the transmission is manual, is it smooth? How does it feel while shifting? Is it too easy to mix up the gears?
♦ If the transmission is automatic, does it shift smoothly and at the right times?
♦ Is the steering responsive at higher speeds? Does it understeer or oversteer around corners?
♦ Do the brakes work smoothly without needing a lot of pressure? Would you feel comfortable in a panic stop?
♦ Is the car quiet when stopped, moving, and accelerating? Turn off the radio to really hear it.
♦ How is the wind noise at higher speeds?
♦ Is the car stable at cruising speeds?
♦ Is the ride too hard or too soft? Do you need a different suspension?
♦ Does it "porpoise" when hitting bumps?
♦ How is the vibration at high speeds and on rougher roads?
♦ Does the engine idle smoothly at stops?
♦ Can it tow anything that you have to tow?
♦ Is this the exact car you are buying or a similar one with significant differences (like a different engine, etc.)?
♦ Is visibility good in all directions? Do you notice any major blind spots?
♦ Are the instruments visible? Can you easily reach all the features, including the radio, windshield wipers, lights, temperature controls, dash, etc.?

THE POST-DRIVE INSPECTION

After you have driven the car and are back at the dealership look at the following:

♦ Will the vehicle fit in your garage?
♦ Is the trunk adequate?
♦ Try the back seat. Is it comfortable, for both sitting and reclining?
♦ Do both front seats recline?
♦ Can you open the hood easily?
♦ Is the motor easily set up for servicing? (This is of particular interest to those of us who change oil, etc.)
♦ Are the oil, water, power steering fluid, etc., marked and easily accessible?

THE FOUR BASIC PARTS OF AN AUTO BUY

Remember, these items must be executed in the *order listed* in order for you to maintain control of the sales situation. These things are done at the dealership with the sales staff *after* all of the homework items have been completed.

♦ Meet the salesperson and take a test drive.
♦ $_____ Get a fixed firm price for your trade-in.
♦ $_____ Set a fixed firm price for the new car and options.
♦ Settle all the financing issues, including payments, leasing, extended warranties, etc.

FINANCING

1. Reaffirm the cost of the new car.
2. Reaffirm the price given you on your trade-in.
3. Reaffirm the amount of down payment needed.
4. Recheck the amount of rebates, first time buyer, etc.
5. Reaffirm the amount of package discounts.
6. Ask about items such as alarm systems.
7. Ask how much time you have before your option to buy an extended warranty expires.
8. Ask about their best financing package before telling them that you have financing from an outside source.

Financing Checklist

1. Lender _____
   interest rate _____% (APR) amount of loan _____
   type of loan _____
2. Lender _____
   interest rate _____% (APR) amount of loan _____
   type of loan _____
3. Dealership _____
   interest rate _____% (APR) amount of loan _____
   type of loan _____
4. Cost of new car (from your negotiations) _____
5. Trade-in value (from your negotiations) _____
6. Down payment (including trade-in) _____
7. Amount of dealer rebate _____
8. Amount of package discounts (luxury package, etc.) _____
9. Amounts of other discounts and rebates (first time buyer, promotional discounts, etc.) _____
10. Sales tax _____% x _____(price) = _____
11. Registration and licensing fees _____
12. Document fee _____
13. Insurance _____
14. Other items (extended warranty, etc.) _____
15. Transportation (freight) _____
16. Dealer's prep (this is usually included at no cost) _____
17. Initial gas and oil (should be included in price) _____
18. Dealer's advertising (I would never pay this one) _____
19. Figure the amount to be financed (4 less 5, 6, 7, 8, and 9 plus 10, 11, 12, 13, 14, 15, and 16) _____
20. Monthly payments for _____ months at _____ APR = _____

LEASING FINANCING CHECKLIST

Remember, negotiate the vehicle price *first,* then discuss leasing. After you decide that you are going to lease you can negotiate such items as interest rate, residual value of the vehicle, etc. Base your lease amount on those figures.

If you are considering leasing, here are some other important questions to ask in financing.

1. What is the interest rate (APR)? _____
2. What is the length of the lease? _____
3. Is the lease figured simple interest? _____
4. What is the interest rate for purchase of the car at the end of the lease? _____
5. What is the price guarantee of the car at the end of the lease? ___ _____
6. Is there any difference between the leasing and buying interest rates? _____
7. Is there any difference between the leasing and buying price or financing? _____
8. Have the dealership spell out the condition the car must be in on return to avoid a penalty. _____
9. What is the maximum mileage per year? Are there penalties for exceeding this? _____
10. How much is the return fee? _____
11. Are there any other fees on return of the car? _____

LEASING CHECKLIST

_____ 1. Interest rate.
_____ 2. Is it an APR or simple interest?
_____ 3. Length of the lease.
_____ 4. Interest rate for purchase of the car at the end of the lease.
_____ 5. Price guarantee of the car at the end of the lease.
_____ 6. Does the interest rate change if I lease or if I buy?
_____ 7. Does the price or financing change if I lease or if I buy?

ITEMS TO DOUBLECHECK

♦ Have you been charged only for items you specifically wanted? (no extras)

♦ Did you get all factory cash, first time buyer's discount, etc?

♦ Was there was anything else promised that the dealer conveniently forgot or nibbled away?

♦ Ask what else they can do for you or give you to make the high cost of the car more palatable. Perhaps they will throw in a cargo net or some sort of an upgrade or a free oil and lube on your first service visit.

♦ Have the finance person write up the contract and put figures on paper. Make sure each figure is explained.

♦ Ask the finance person if anything was added to the pricing of the car that you did not specifically request, but that he thought you might need or want.

♦ Is the car a refugee from the lemon law?

♦ Is the car a flood car?

♦ Is the car damaged, was it in an accident and fixed up?

♦ Is there anything about the car that I should know about in order to make an informed decision?

♦ Have there been any recalls on this type of car? What type?

♦ What is the length of guarantee on this car?

♦ Does the dealership provide loaner cars or transportation if the car needs covered repairs?

♦ Is the car really new? Has it ever been registered before?

♦ Did you get everything you asked for? Has anything been omitted or held back? (Check your list made during negotiations.)

♦ Doublecheck all of the numbers used to price your car (in case of inadvertent substitution or error).

♦ If there are repairs or substitutions promised you, hold back a part of the money until they are completed or else refuse to sign until they are completed.

♦ Check to make sure that no fees were tacked on after the final figure has been decided upon (such as dealer's prep fee which usually is included in the price of the car).

♦ Ask for them to throw in some free floor mats when you sign.

USED CAR PHONE QUERY CHECKLIST

First ask, "Are you a dealer or a private party?" _____

Car type _____

Year _____

Mileage _____

   Is the mileage real? _____

Engine size _____

Number of doors _____

Type of transmission — stick or automatic _____

Special model or style _____

Color _____

Interior condition _____

Exterior condition _____

Asking price _____

   Is this price negotiable? _____

Power steering _____

Power brakes _____

Cruise control _____

Tilt steering _____

Power seat _____

Leather seats _____

Safety equipment _____

   air bags _____

   antilock brakes _____

Sound system _____

   regular am/fm _____

   cassette deck _____

   compact disk _____

   other premium sound items _____

Special light group _____

Special luxury group _____

Special wheels _____

Special tires _____

Floor pads _____

Are the service records available? _____

Is the car title on hand? _____

Is there any lien holder on the vehicle? _____

Has the car ever been in an accident? _____

Other questions or comments _____

Additional Questions

1. Why are you selling the car? _____
2. Are you the original owner? _____
3. What is wrong with the car? _____
4. If this is a recreational vehicle, has it ever been offroaded or rolled? _____
5. Is the price negotiable? _____
6. What is the bottom-line price? _____
7. Where exactly are you located? _____
8. How is the body condition? _____
    Has the car been in any accidents? _____
    Is there any rust? _____
9. How new are the tires? _____
    Do you still have the receipts and warranty? _____
10. Will you guarantee the car? _____
11. How long has the car been on the market? _____
12. Has the car had any recent repairs? _____
    Do you still have the service records? _____
13. (Ask again) What price do you need for the car? _____
    Would you consider $_____ below that price? _____
14. Do you own the car outright or is there still money owed on it? _____
15. Are you in a hurry to sell the car? _____
16. Have you had a mechanic look at your car since you put it on the market? _____
    Is it a problem if I have my mechanic look it over? _____
17. How good is the paint? _____
18. What is the Blue Book retail and wholesale for the car? _____
19. Will you pay for the smogging or smog inspection and any work necessary to pass the testing if the car fails the inspection? _____
20. When was the last tuneup? _____
    If it has been a while, ask: Will you pay for a tuneup? _____
    If not, will you pay half the cost of a tuneup? _____
21. Is the car registered in your state? _____
22. Ask anything else that interests you. Remember, you don't know what you will find out or what they may give away. _____
23. Try to get the seller to talk price concessions over the phone. ___

EVALUATING A USED CAR

Exterior

1. Is there any broken or pitted glass?
2. Is the paint in good condition?
3. Are there any indications of a repaint job? Good clues include: orange peel texture, over-spray painting on chrome, rubber, door jambs, or under the hood, and mismatched paints. Signs of a repaint job are usually signs of an accident.
4. Is there any major structural damage? Look for wavy body panels or mismatched colors of paint. Use a magnet (one of those soft refrigerator ones) and check to make sure that all body parts are metal. Often accidents are repaired used a non-metal called Bondo® as fill material. The magnet will reveal its presence. Look in the trunk and under the pads in the back for any indications of corrected rear end damage.
5. Is there any minor structural damage? Look for loose trim, bent side mirrors, missing antennas, missing gas caps, broken door handles, loose bumpers, etc.
6. Is there damage to the paint? Look for door dings, paint scratches, and fading or peeling paint.
7. Are the headlights and tail lights intact? Do they work properly? What about the signals?
8. Are the floor mats with the vehicle?
9. Ask if the car has been garaged during its lifetime. See if the answer meshes with the condition of the car.
10. If the car is a four-wheel drive, ask if it has been offroaded. Look for evidence that it has been offroaded. Dings, especially roof damage, are strong evidence of offroading.
11. How are the tires? Look for good tread and even wear. If they are worn unevenly, they may need to be aligned or replaced. Put your hands on the tires; if the tread is cupped, you may have a strut or shock problem.

Also note if the tire rims are upscale or base rims. If the car has base rims, ask if you can have the upscale rims if he has any.

Anybody with a good eye can check the exterior and thus get a good indication of the care and maintenance of the car. It should be relatively easy to spot evidence of prior neglect or an accident.

Interior

The goal of inspecting the interior is two-fold. You want to see if the vehicle has been abused and you also want to see if you feel comfortable inside the car.

1. Are the seats in good shape? Look at the seat material. Is it ripped, soiled, or otherwise undesirable? Does the padding look deformed? Was the previous owner extremely heavy, making the seat unusable for you?
2. Sit in the seat and close the doors. Close your eyes and inhale. Do you get a good feeling, or do you feel uneasy?
3. Sit in the back seats. Check the seating material and details in the back.
4. How is the odor? Is there residual odor of abuse (vomit, beer, solvents, etc.). If you are a non-smoker and the seller smoked heavily, this may be a deterrent to you. You might use this as a negotiating point. You can always bargain for the money needed to get a good detailing job done to remove odors. Do this only if the odor is bearable, as there is no guarantee that detailing will take care of the problem.
5. Look for wear and tear that is not consistent with the mileage on the car. Torn seats or very worn pedals and armrests on a car that shows 32,000 miles is an indication that perhaps the mileage has been altered.
6. Do the window cranks or power windows work?
7. Check the lights and turn signals with someone on the outside. Also check the horn. If only you and the seller are present, ask him/her to try the signals while you check them from the outside.
8. Do the window wipers/washers work? Check front and back.
9. Do the seats move smoothly and easily?
10. Does the radio work? Check all the speakers. Note the stations that are fixed in memory. If it is a Spanish station and the seller is not, ask (again) if he is a dealer and not the original owner.
11. Start the engine and turn on the air conditioning. It should run cold. If not, assume the worst, repairing a frozen compressor will cost at least $500. Make sure the fan runs. If you know what you are doing, check to see if the compressor is frozen or if it is something simple like a broken belt.
12. Do all of the interior panels light up? Do all of the interior lights work? Are all the plastic covers in place?
13. Is the dashboard in good condition?
14. Is the steering wheel bent? This may indicate an accident.

15. With the car in park (neutral for a stick shift) run the engine very high for five seconds and notice what comes out the tailpipe. Be ready to walk away if the smoke is heavy white or blue. An initial transient blue puff of smoke on a car that has been sitting for a long while may indicate a valve seal problem.

16. Are there any missing small parts? Check knobs, window cranks, ashtray covers, etc.

17. Ask about the mileage again. Is this the original mileage or has the odometer been replaced or altered? If you have any doubts, have them guarantee the validity of the odometer reading in writing.

18. Look in the glove box for the manual, recent repair bills, etc. Ask what has been done to the car recently.

Mechanical

These are things you can check even if you are not a professional mechanic. If you spot something that may be indicative of trouble, you will be able to ask your mechanic about it.

1. Check the oil. If it is brand new, you learn nothing except that the seller had the oil changed to enhance the selling chances.

2. Look for a gelatinous goop around the inside of the oil fill cap or in the oil chamber. This may indicate a water leak. Be prepared to walk away at this point. Hard caked muddy oil on a dipstick indicates that the oil in the past may not have been changed frequently. If the present oil is clean but the cap is muddy, the oil was changed to cover up the problem. When inspecting the oil, look for metal flakes or grit in the oil. If any are observed, be concerned.

3. Look for evidence of oil leakage on engine surfaces. Ask where the car is normally parked and look for oil there. You will need a mechanic to evaluate if it is serious. With the car in park and the idle low, look at the pressure gauge: if the oil pressure is low there may be an oil pump problem.

4. Look for fluid leaking onto such items as brakes, etc.

5. Check the radiator water. See if the antifreeze is new or if it is rust colored.

6. If the car has been sitting and is not hot, run your fingers around the inside of the tailpipe and see what comes out on them. If it is carbon and water, you are okay (maybe you need a tuneup). If it is oily, be careful. Do not put your fingers *near* the tailpipe if the car has been running; it gets very hot.

7. Check the belts and see if they are tight. If they look frayed or the edges are white, you may have some work to do.

8. Listen for noises. The engine should start and run quietly; if there is too much engine vibration there may be problems. A tapping or banging sound spells trouble. Any spraying of oil or water is bad news.
9. Check out the gears. All of them (forward and reverse) should work, and they should shift quietly. Check for pickup and power.
10. Check the transmission fluid. It should be pink. If it is yellow or brown and smells burnt, take it as evidence of major transmission problems.
11. With the car in drive, use the lowest amount of gas and see if the transmission slips.
12. At speed, slam on the brakes (warn your passenger first) and see how the car stops. There should be no squeaking and the vehicle should stop quickly in a straight line. Any bumping indicates the brakes are about shot.

NEGOTIATING POINTS

It is very legitimate to ask for price reductions to compensate for defects. Make sure that you compile a list during your inspection. It will prove invaluable when you begin negotiations with the seller.

1. Repair work that has to be done.
2. Tires that have to be replaced.
3. Alignment or balancing that must be done.
4. Door dings or paint imperfections that must be corrected.
5. Seats that must be reupholstered.
6. Carpeting rips.
7. Replacement of missing knobs, bulbs, parts, etc.
8. Was the car in a fender bender or worse?
9. What kind of repair work or general maintenance has been done on the car?
10. Who has been driving the car — a kid, an older person?
11. Mileage and perhaps mileage discrepancies.

USED CAR SMALL TALK CHECKLIST

1. Is he the real seller?
2. Why is he selling the vehicle?
3. Is he comfortable selling the vehicle?
4. What does he need from this transaction?
5. How long has he been trying to sell this vehicle?
6. What is his real bottom line?
7. What can you trade off to get a better price?
8. Does he own the car, or does a bank or finance company?
9. Does he need to sell the car quickly to get money for a new vehicle?
10. Is he the type who can handle the sale and continually negotiate without getting his feelings bent out of shape?

A complete catalog of Betterway Books is available FREE by writing to the address shown below, or by calling toll-free 1-800-289-0963. To order additional copies of this book, send in retail price of the book plus $3.00 postage and handling for one book, and $1.00 for each additional book. Ohio residents add 5½% sales tax. Allow 30 days for delivery.

Betterway Books
1507 Dana Avenue
Cincinnati, Ohio 45207

Index